C000172538

*"So I have a message
for our friends in Europe:
We will walk with you, talk with you,
Buy with you, sell with you,
But we will be damned if we
will be governed by you!"*

From my speech to Party
Conference, Oct 1998.
With acknowledgements to
Shakespeare and Shylock!

Dedication

I'd like to dedicate this slim volume to my comrade-in-arms
Christopher Heaton-Harris, an East Midlands MEP from 1999
to 2009, and now MP for Daventry. It was a pleasure to work
alongside Chris for the first ten years of my parliamentary
career, and I am hugely grateful to him for his support and
friendship. Brussels' loss is Daventry's gain.

Acknowledgements

I need to thank several people. First I must thank Jonathan Isaby for permission to reuse here articles and comments that I first published on the excellent ConservativeHome blog, which can be found on http://conservativehome.blogs.com/. ConHome is required reading for any Conservative. I am grateful to Simon Richards and The Freedom Association for a long, happy and productive working relationship. I also need to thank my editor, Rupert Matthews of Bretwalda Books, who has helped me to put this book together.

First Published 2011
Copyright © Roger Helmer 2011

All rights reserved. No reproduction of any part of this publication is permitted without the prior written permission of the publisher:

Bretwalda Books
Unit 8, Fir Tree Close, Epsom,
Surrey KT17 3LD

info@BretwaldaBooks.com

To receive an e-catalogue of our complete range of books send an email to info@BretwaldaBooks.com

ISBN 978-1-907791-20-8

Foreword
by Rt Hon John Redwood MP

*R*oger Helmer revels in controversy. For most it would be
sufficient to take on the mighty battalions of the European
federalists, something Roger has been doing to an ever greater
extent. As a sceptic at large Roger Helmer also takes on the
massed ranks of the global warming exponents, denying that
the climate is warming much and refuting the idea that if it is
it is the result of human creations of CO_2. As a result he is often
vilified by two strongly entrenched establishments who do not
like disagreement or an alternative view.

On the European issues he recounts how he undertook a U
turn, from thinking the UK could reform its position within
the EU from within, to believing that the UK has to leave the
EU to restore its sovereignty and to follow the policies it wishes.
Watching the tortuous negotiations of the EU Constitution,
seeing the votes in France and Denmark against it, and then
seeing something similar reappear and carry, offended his
democratic sense. Roger's journey as he spent more time in EU
politics was counter flow. Where many might have come to
appreciate the lifestyle and to be influenced by the federalist
arguments that support it, Roger grew angrier about the tide of
political power washing to Brussels.

When it came to climate change, as a mathematician he
tried to understand the famous hockey stick graph which
purported to show that the climate had been very stable for
centuries, and that suddenly there has been a sharp and
sustained acceleration in warming. Roger did not think the
figures or conventional climate history bore this out, and led
him to doubt the whole theory. He disagreed that the
phenomenon was happening on the scale claimed, denied that
any warming was the result of human action rather than sun

spots or other natural events, and decried the proposed remedies from the EU and other governments. Where Nigel Lawson concentrated on explaining the economics, arguing that trying to stop global emissions today was not the most cost effective or sensible way of tackling the problem, Roger denied it all root and branch.

Our national debate is the richer for a sceptic at large. Roger puts establishments on their mettle, challenges other politicians to think about the preconceptions they share with governments, and offers challenging views to the public.

Best Wishes,

The Rt Hon John Redwood MP
Member of Parliament for Wokingham

A Sceptical Introduction

This book has been a long time coming.

As a former mathematician who has spent part of his career in science-based industries, I have always seen the merits of a sceptical approach. Science is impossible without scepticism -- it goes with the territory. Scientists are supposed to be sceptical -- or at least they were when I was in Cambridge in the 60s.

So I started out fairly sceptical about the EU. But it took years in the European parliament to convince me that the EU was beyond reform, that it deserved to be put out of its misery. I had originally accepted the Party's position that while there was much wrong in Europe, our task was to get in there and to sort it out. Were our politicians and civil servants not as good as theirs? Could we not win the arguments in Brussels? Wasn't reform a realistic objective?

Yet we had been members since 1973, and like a dinosaur in a tar pit we just kept getting deeper in. We had been talking about reform ever since we started out, yet the EU's commitment to ever-closer-union remained. Each new EU Treaty transferred more powers to Europe. I found it more and more difficult to justify the Party's position that membership was in Britain's interests when it so obviously was not, or to argue for reform when attempts at reform had been failing for decades.

ABOVE: In my office at EuroParl in Brussels.

I realised at last that we should be Better Off Out. So I took a deep breath and decided to say so.

I have recently been hounded by a Guardian journalist so incensed by my views and actions that he has become something of a cyber-stalker. No matter where my virtual self turns on the web, there he is with his virtual notebook in hand. And he is but the most persistent of a number of journalists who have dogged my steps since my U-turn. They have crawled over my accounts trying to find something irregular (in vain I might add). They have trawled my speeches and articles to find isolated words and phrases that they can twist in an effort to demonise me and misrepresent my views.

Not all the brickbats have come from the left. Since I took a clear position on the EU, calling for Britain to leave, and especially since I started challenging the conventional wisdom on climate issues, I have had one or two challenges from the Tory ranks as well. But a Party like the Conservative party is necessarily a broad church, and lively debate on vital issues is surely at the heart of politics. Nonetheless I do sometimes wonder how the Conservative Party which I joined seems these days to find it so easy to adopt remarkably un-conservative positions.

It has been a bit hard going at times, but I make no complaints. I put my head over the parapet. And in any case, it has been worth it.

Before moving on to the reasons for my change of heart, why it has proved to be so profound and what has happened since then, I think I had better sketch in a bit of background.

I will try to be brief. I was born in London in January 1944. My first months were passed with German V1 flying bombs rattling overhead and plunging down to blast houses to pieces.

Fortunately I remember nothing of such horrors. By the time I was at school we had moved to Southampton, where I attended King Edward VI School. I then gained a state scholarship (one of the last) to Churchill College, Cambridge. I read mathematics, something which encouraged a rigorous and analytical way of thinking. Entering business, I worked for a number of companies over the years including Procter & Gamble, National Semiconductor, Coats Viyella and the whisky firm United Distillers (now Diageo). I lived and worked in Hong Kong, Singapore, Thailand, Malaysia and Korea, and ran businesses in the Philippines, Vietnam, Guam and Saipan.

So, having covered 55 years in a single paragraph, we come to my entry into politics and the countdown to my conversion from sceptic to Sceptic at Large. In the summer of 1998 I had the honour to be chosen as the No.1 candidate for the Conservative Party in the East Midlands Region of England for the European Elections due to be held in June 1999. Given the odd closed list proportional voting system used in elections for the European Union, this meant I was almost certain to be elected. I gave up my paid employment and campaigned full time over the following months. I had been a member of the party for decades, of course, and had played my part in fund raising and other events, but until this date had never seriously contemplated running for office.

I learned early on that most people across the East Midlands shared my suspicion of the EU project to create a unitary superstate – we called it Federalism back then I seem to recall. They also backed my stance against the pointless bureaucracy, red tape and interference from Brussels. Few of them had a good word to say for the endemic corruption and incompetence so typical of the EU. And that was back in 1998!

So in 1999 I was first elected as an MEP. I railed against EU corruption, criticised EU integration and sought to understand how such obviously undemocratic institutions could be supported by so many apparently clever people. Looking back I was something of a bright-eyed newcomer. Certainly some of the old hands thought of me as somebody who would learn. I did. But not in the way they wanted.

I had barely been an MEP for two years before the great and the good in the EU reached a decision at Laeken. At the time there were a number of east European countries queuing up to join the EU — Poland, the Czech Republic, Bulgaria, Estonia, Hungary, Lithuania, Latvia, Slovakia, Slovenia and Romania — plus Cyprus and Malta from the Mediterranean. The influx of so many new member states would, it was argued, put a strain on the existing structures of the EU. Reform was therefore needed.

I had no argument with that. It seemed no more than commonsense. What made this move rather more promising was that the Laeken meeting recognised that there were problems with democracy, transparency and efficiency within the EU and its institutions. They could have added

corruption so far as I was concerned, but even so it appeared that those at the top of the EU project had got the message that something was wrong and it needed putting right.

That chimed exactly with my views at the time. The EU had the potential to achieve much good, but was failing to do so due to a range of problems with the institutions of the EU and the people who worked there. Reform was also the policy of the Conservative Party, and one that I was proud and eager to support.

So Laeken set up a European Convention chaired by the former French President Valery Giscard d'Estaing. Its task was to look at the various problems and come up with a solution. The Convention was made up of MPs from each member state, MEPs, and other assorted representatives. Deliberately or otherwise the European Convention mirrored the Continental Convention, which in 1787 produced the Constitution of the USA. A happy role model, I thought, for the cause of liberty.

How wrong I was.

At once the way in which the EU likes to do business got to work. Giscard d'Estaing began by forming a Praesidium of 15 people. This inner core had the real decision-making power. Unsurprisingly d'Estaing ensured that only those who agreed with his views sat on the Praesidium. Those who did not toe the line were shunted off to "working groups" that talked endlessly and enjoyed some jolly nice lunches, but had no real power.

The Praesidium chose to ignore the problems of democracy, transparency and efficiency (never mind corruption) that it had been tasked with solving. Instead it chose to focus on the administrative problems expected to be caused by the new member states. And the solution it suggested was a new all-embracing Constitution for the European Union. This would replace the succession of treaties that until then had governed how the EU ran itself. At the same time it would both give the EU a legal personality for the first time and transfer large tranches of power from the member states to the EU itself. In June 2004 the final text was agreed, but it needed to be ratified before it came into operation.

Effectively it would end British independence.

I was not prepared to put up with that. Fortunately, the Conservative Party at the time had a policy of insisting on a

BELOW: When I was in Riga, in March 2010 I went to the Esplanade to pay homage to that great Latvian playwright, politician and nationalist Janis Plieksans. His brand of patriotism was unpopular with the multi-national dictatorship (sound familiar?) of the Tsars so he wrote under the name of Rainis by which he is better known.

ABOVE: With my office staff in the autumn of 2010. From left to right: Joseph Bono my researcher, Neelam Cartmell my press officer, me, Elisa Nolte a stagière who was with us for a few months, Lydia Smith my office manager.

referendum of the British people before the new EU Constitution could be agreed. The issue proved to be of some (though not dominating) importance at the UK General Election held in May 2005. Labour was pushed into making a similar referendum pledge. When Labour won the election, that promise thus became government policy. No precise date was set for the referendum. I suspected that Mr Blair would leave it until after all the other EU member states had voted in the hope that either one of the others would vote No or, if that did not happen, that a tidal wave of momentum for a Yes would have built up to wash the British public in its wake.

I had more faith in the British public than that. I knew they would not be bullied or bamboozled. I knew that they would vote No. I suspect Mr Blair knew that too.

In the event, of course, it never got that far. The Spanish voted Yes, but then the French voted No by 55% to 45% on 29 May 2005 and three days later the Dutch voted No by a margin of almost two to one. The EU Constitution appeared to be dead. But like Dracula of old, it was to rise from the dead.

The EU élite formed themselves into what they called the Amato Group, led by former Italian Prime Minister Giuliano Amato and composed of ministers and ex-ministers from the EU member states. All were fully signed up to the EU Project of creating a superstate. None of them was elected.

This group set out, with wonderful cynicism, to create a new Treaty which, when taken together with the existing treaties, would deliver, in effect, everything that was in the failed Constitution. They chopped and changed paragraphs, but used most of the text from the Constitution in the new document. They presented it as a series of amendments to earlier treaties, without giving the context, so that unless readers were prepared to cross-reference the new text with the existing treaties, it was incomprehensible. And they re-numbered paragraphs in successive drafts, further obfuscating the meaning.

Jens-Peter Bonde, then an MEP with the EU democrats, produced a reader-friendly version of the treaty, bringing together the original texts as amended, and I commend this to anyone who wants to understand it further. Find it at http://www.eudemocrats.org/fileadmin/u ser_upload/Documents/D-Reader_friendly_latest%20version.pdf

We in Britain were told that the new Treaty was quite different from the failed Constitution, and therefore that the earlier promise of a Constitutional referendum was null and void. After all, we had not had referendums on previous treaties – so why on this one? In one sense it *was* different. Whereas the Constitution would have replaced a cat's-cradle of historical treaties with a new, single document, arguably bringing greater clarity, the new treaty would stand alongside and modify the previous treaties. The mendacity arose because although the Lisbon Treaty technically represented a different approach, the outcome was (and was designed to be) exactly the same. So while our Labour government was assuring us that the Treaty was quite different from the Constitution, successive European luminaries were coming forward to claim that the new text was 95% -- no, 98% -- no, 99% identical. They out-bid each other day after day. Giscard d'Estaing himself, the progenitor of the failed Constitution, said he could find no substantive difference in the new text.

The only difference which I could recognise was that the "symbols of statehood" -- the flag and the anthem -- had now been omitted, in deference to eurosceptic sensibilities. But as they continued to be used exactly as before, this was a distinction without a difference.

That was when I committed one of the worst offences that a politician can be accused of. I changed my mind, or as they say in the tabloids, I did a U-turn. Until then I had believed, as the Conservative Party believed, that the EU was capable of reform, and that our task was to stay in and reform it. Our job was to win the arguments in Brussels, and to create an EU in which Britain could be comfortable, and where our independence and self governance could be assured. On this basis, I was quite happy with our very successful 1999 campaign slogan "In Europe, not Run by Europe".

But during my years in Brussels I had gradually been coming to realise that this was not a viable policy. Many times I had seen us win the arguments in Brussels, only to lose the votes. There was, and remains, an in-built majority in favour of a centralised, harmonised European state.

Now, with the report of the Amato Group I realised that trying to get the EU to change direction is like getting on a bus from Derby to Edinburgh, and trying to persuade the driver and passengers that they would really rather to go to London instead. But they don't want to go to London. You have to recognise sooner or later that you got on the wrong bus. The EU bus is going towards ever closer union. We can either go along or get off.

I and many others had known for some time that the EU is costing us far more, in direct contributions and in regulatory costs, than any possible benefit we get out of it. The new Lisbon Treaty (the old EU Constitution in a new package) was going to make matters worse, would consolidate powers in the EU and destroy the legal basis of British independence as a sovereign state. I realised that the EU is beyond reform, and deserves to be put out of its misery.

That is why I signed up to the Better Off Out campaign, sponsored by the Freedom Association, an organisation of which I then had the privilege to be Honorary Chairman. That was my U-turn. And I am proud of it.

Since then I have been fighting the good fight on many fronts. Looking back on the past four years or so I see that I have chronicled that fight on my website, in press releases, in speeches, in tweets and above all on my blog.

This book is the story of what has happened since my decision to say openly that Britain would be Better Off Out. I have chosen to tell the story with the aid of what I wrote at the time, with some explanatory text to set my comments in context.

Hindsight is a wonderful thing, and politicians use it more often than most. I have taken the brave (some have told me foolish) decision to eschew it here. This book is mostly made up of what I wrote at the time. Sometimes I was right, sometimes I was wrong, but either way it is here. You can be the judge. Decide whether, on balance, I was generally correct, generally wrong or generally on a different planet.

I have also included a final chapter giving my thoughts on the future. Making predictions is notoriously difficult – especially about the future as Mark Twain said. If eschewing hindsight is brave, surely making predictions is foolhardy. Never mind. It is enjoyable.

So take up this book and follow me on my journey. As they say: "Fasten your seat belts. This is going to be a bumpy ride."

A Sceptic on the EU

As an MEP most of my waking life is taken up by the EU and its various organs. Like some demented octopus, it is capable of pushing its tentacles in to nooks and crannies where it is not only not wanted but where it has no business going. In the rest of the book, I will be looking at other policy areas where I have got involved and the ways in which my parting of the ways with the EU have influenced my views and actions.

But since I am an MEP and since my work is mostly concerned with the EU, I had better start there. And I make no excuses for making this the longest chapter in the book.

I will start back in February 2007 when the infamous Amato Group was still huddled in its meetings. It had not yet produced its appalling plan to defy democracy in the most blatant and authoritarian way by pushing ahead with the defeated EU Constitution under a new name "The Lisbon Treaty". But enough information had leaked out to give an indication of where things were going.

BELOW: In 2005 Chris Heaton-Harris and I signed an open letter to British Prime Minister, Antony Blair, demanding a referendum in Britain on the European Constitution.

twitter

Tragedy in Smith Square: The former CCHQ is now the headquarters of the Occupying Power

In February 2007 I wrote the following:

A slap in the face for Democracy

Back in 2005, the French people voted by a substantial margin to reject the European Constitution, and days later the Dutch rejected it by an even larger margin. The document contained its own ratification criteria. It required all countries to ratify, yet two major EU founder-members rejected it.

If democracy means anything, the constitution is dead. The people have spoken. But the European élites were not going to give up so easily. They declared a pause for reflection, although (as Quentin Letts said in the FT) it has proved to be all pause and no reflection. And now, without a backward glance at the voters of France and Holland, President-in-Office Angela Merkel is determined to carry through the original document, with no more than cosmetic changes, and have it in place before the 2009 euro-elections.

We hear the EU described as "A union of values based on democracy and the rule of law". Yet Merkel demonstrates a contempt for democracy and for the will of the electorate that is simply breathtaking in its scale.

But of course the EU has form in this area. Twice before, in Denmark in 1992 and Ireland in 2001, it simply rejected the result of a referendum and required the people to vote again. This is 'biased finality' in action: "you can vote how you like, so long as you get the right answer. And if you get the wrong answer, you can just keep on voting until you do what we want."

Yet this latest abuse of process is on an unprecedented scale. Both Denmark and Ireland are relatively small countries who joined well after the Treaty of Rome. Holland and France are both founder-members, and France at least is one of the largest. If the verdicts of their electorates can be ignored, then clearly the EU's élites believe they can do no wrong. The divine right of Kings has become the divine right of Brussels .

But there is a development here that the EU ignores at its peril. The French vote has validated euroscepticism. In France, we see the establishment, the media, and the politicians almost without exception backing the European project. Any individual Frenchman harbouring doubts about the EU must have must have felt isolated and marginalised -- why did he alone have these doubts when apparently no one else had?

But now these isolated sceptics have woken up to find that they are a majority. And there is no doubt that Germany and the UK , given the

opportunity, would also vote NO. Indeed I have heard Spanish MEPs saying that if the Spanish referendum were to be repeated now, following the French and Dutch votes, then Spain would also vote NO.

The genie is out of the bottle, and cannot be put back. Now the Commission is complaining that the EU has become "a lightning rod" for general dissatisfaction. They are right. Some might feel that it well deserves the role.

There is a game being played by politicians and commentators about what the voters "really meant" by voting NO. They were worried about globalisation. They feared Turkish immigration. They were venting their dissatisfaction with national leaders. No one seems to have considered the possibility that the voters had simply been offered more Europe , and said "No Thanks".

In the UK , a former Minister for Europe is now saying that we should have no more referenda because "voters never answer the question on the ballot paper". Contempt for democracy is not limited to Germany .

There are clear signs now of a real split in the European project. There are countries that want Constitution Plus, that want to move on to full political and economic union. There are others in Eastern Europe, Scandinavia and the UK who see the benefits of trade and cooperation, but are fretting under the

weight of EU regulation and the threat of political centralisation.

The case for variable geometry has never been stronger. Let those who want to submerge their nations into a United States of Europe be free to do so. Let the rest negotiate terms which best suit themselves. Call it Associate Membership. For my country, I want to see a relationship based solely on free trade and voluntary intergovernmental cooperation.

Looking back, I fear that I was being rather optimistic here. I was still groping my way towards my epiphany. I still hoped that the EU could be reformed from within. I was wrong.

The process rumbled on. On 21 June 2007 the European Council met in Brussels and announced a mandate for an Intergovernmental Conference to decide on the new treaty, as proposed by Amato. That IGC met in Lisbon on 23 July and rubberstamped the plan, which thus formally became the draft Lisbon Treaty. On 7 September the EU member states' Foreign Ministers met and agreed the draft text, which then went to the European Council meeting in Lisbon on 18 October. With minor changes the text was agreed and on 13 December 2007 was signed in Lisbon by the heads of government.

It was announced that the Lisbon Treaty would come into force on 1 January 2009. Any pretence of democracy was dropped when the governments one by one announced that the referenda promised for the EU

Constitution would not be held on the Lisbon Treaty. This was on the specious grounds that the two were different documents. In fact they were so similar as to be identical in every possible meaning of the word.

I was not the only one to perform a U-turn over the EU because of this. British Labour MP Gisela Stuart was a member of the Convention which drafted the original Constitution. She arrived in Brussels a starry-eyed Europhile – "German by birth and British by choice" – but was soon to be disabused, as she came to understand that she was there merely to give a spurious veneer of democratic legitimacy to the process, but that no one was prepared to listen to her views. She wrote an excellent booklet for the Fabian Society, "The Making of Europe's Constitution". In it, she mentions that her spell-check repeatedly tried to replace "Giscard" with "discard". Very apt.

On 20 February 2008 the Lisbon Treaty came to the EU Parliament. Due to the complexities of EU Parliamentary procedure it was dubbed "The Corbett Report" as the MEP who guided the matter through the preliminary committee stage was one Richard Corbett, Labour MEP for the Yorkshire and the Humber Region.

Corbett has long had a reputation for wanting to strengthen the powers of the EU. No doubt his known adherence to the EU Project explains why he was chosen for the task of taking the Lisbon Treaty through the EU Parliament. Clearly, however, the voters he purports to represent were not so impressed. At the 2009 EU Elections he lost his seat to the BNP. But the EU looks after their own. His reward came in the form of a job in the Cabinet of President Rumpy-Pumpy, of which more later.

When the Corbett Report came to the EU Parliamentary Plenary Session (when we all get to vote on things) I was delighted to get the chance to speak in the debate on 20th February 2008. Here is what I said:

Mr. President

Today, the European project abandons any claim to democratic legitimacy. Today we will vote through the Renamed Constitution, in an act that shows monstrous contempt for European citizens and Democratic values.

In 2005, the voters of France and Holland decisively rejected the Constitution. I am astonished by the bare-faced effrontery of European leaders who have changed the packaging, but are now bringing back the rejected substance in defiance of public opinion.

Most French and Dutch MEPs will support this report. I do not know how they will face their voters. I do not know how they will sleep at night.

In the UK, our Labour government has broken its solemn promise of a referendum. Yet in postal polls conducted by campaign groups, more than 80% of voters vote YES to a referendum.

By forcing through this measure in the teeth of public opposition, you are hacking at the very foundations of the Europe you are trying to build. We must listen to the people. We demand a referendum.

━━━━━━━━━ twitter 🐦

Brendan O'Neill: Listening to Catherine Ashton give a lecture about democracy is a bit like listening to Quasimodo dish out beauty tips

Time is very limited at Plenary. Generally you get only 60 seconds to talk. I am not normally so reticent. The Plenary saw an amendment moved calling on the EU to respect the result of the then imminent Irish referendum in a way that they had not done for the French and Dutch referenda of 2005. That led to an amusing, and yet disgraceful, fall out some days later. I was present for the event and on 11 March 2008 blogged on the event as follows:

The Sophistry of Richard Corbett

During the parliament's February Strasbourg session, we voted the Corbett report on the Lisbon Treaty (aka the Renamed EU Constitution). There was an amendment that simply said "This house will recognise the outcome of the Irish Referendum". The amendment was overwhelmingly voted down.

In a meeting of the Constitutional Affairs Committee yesterday, we were discussing the poor turnout in Euro-elections, and the apparent voter disengagement from the European project. Irish MEP Kathy Sinnott pointed out that we could hardly expect Irish voters to engage with the EU when we had just voted against respecting the result of the Irish Referendum. Corbett was apoplectic, shouting "No we didn't" (I was shouting "Yes you did") and insisting on making a point of order in response. His explanation was about the most extraordinary piece of self-serving sophistry that I have heard in nearly nine years in the parliament (and I've heard a lot!).

We weren't voting to reject the outcome of the Irish referendum, he said. Not at all. We were merely voting not to put that wording into the text of the report. And why did we not want to put those words in the report? Why, said Corbett, because "It is self-evident that this parliament would respect the outcome of any national referendum -- not just Ireland".

I have rarely seen an MEP dig himself an elephant-trap, and fall into it quite so quickly. Self-evident, is it? The European parliament was quite happy to reject the Danish referendum on Maastricht (1992); the Irish Referendum on the Nice Treaty (2000); and most spectacularly the French and Dutch referendum results on the EU Constitution in 2005. Self-evident that we respect the result of national referenda, Richard? No. It's self-evident that we don't.

17

In my short intervention following Corbett, I reminded the Committee (how they hated it!) that while some 80% of MEPs had voted for the Corbett Report supporting the Lisbon Treaty, a large-scale postal ballot in the UK with a stunning response rate (for a private referendum) of 36%+ had voted 89% against the Lisbon Treaty. The parliament will reject that as well. The Constitutional Affairs Committee is trying to read the tea-leaves to find why turnout is drifting down in European elections. They could start to solve the problem by listening to the people.

ABOVE: It is usually considered the height of bad manners in the EU Parliament to so much as mention "The War", so it was with some amazement that I came across this exhibition inside the Parliament building itself that was dedicated to our heroic RAF who fought during the Battle of Britain. I think the organisers managed to get away with it as they were actually highlighting British-Czech co-operation and in particular the gallant role of the 88 Czech pilots during the battle.

Things were now moving fast. The private referendum to which I had referred was held in Britain. A cross-party organisation called "IWantAReferendum.Com" organised a series of postal ballots in constituencies across the country. All voters registered for general elections received a ballot paper. For a privately organised vote the response rate was quite astonishing – nudging 40% in some places – and compared well to turnout for local elections. In my own East Midlands region it was Gedling that got the chance to vote on whether or not there should be a referendum on the Lisbon Treaty. The good folk of Gedling turned out in impressive numbers with 40% voting, more than in some local elections. Of those 21,000 votes cast, a massive 87% voted for a referendum. I am sure that they would have voted No to Lisbon if they had ever been given the chance.

One of the more bizarre features about the procedures of the EU Parliament (and trust me there are many bizarre features) is that once an MEP has been thrown out of a party group he or she gets one very useful benefit. He or she gets to speak in Plenary Sessions far more often than do MEPs in party groupings. At this date I was in the Conservative Party, but I was outside the European Peoples Party (EPP) grouping to which the Conservatives belong. In EU Parliament speak I was "non-inscrit". So against the odds, I got another speech at the next Plenary Session of the Parliament in March. I chose to speak on the postal ballots organised by IWantAReferendum.Com.

Mr. President,

The ratification of the Renamed EU Constitution threatens the democratic legitimacy of the European project itself. The peoples of France and Holland rejected the Constitution. Yet it has now come back with a new name, and with what Angela Merkel called "cosmetic changes".

Now the institutions and the member-states, including the Labour government in the UK, are dishonestly pretending that these cosmetic changes justify breaking their promise of a referendum. They do not, and the pretence that they do is a huge breach of faith with the people.

In Britain, a campaign group has just undertaken an independently monitored postal ballot in ten Westminster constituencies. Over 150,000 voters responded. 88% want a referendum. 89% oppose the Treaty. In six constituencies, more people voted for a referendum than voted for their current member of parliament.

The people have spoken. The Treaty cannot be legitimate without their consent. The European Council must listen. We must have a referendum.

On 13th March, the day after I spoke at the Plenary, I made my feelings clear on my website.

EU Anthem: dead but it won't lie down

The European Parliament meeting at Strasbourg yesterday celebrated its 50th birthday with a concert, at which the European flag was flown, and the European National Anthem (Beethoven's 9th Symphony) played. Our Labour government has tried to justify its decision to deny a referendum on the new EU Treaty by arguing that the Treaty has dropped the flag and the anthem, the "Constitutional Elements" of the failed EU Constitution -- yet the flag still flies, and the anthem is still played. German Chancellor Angela Merkel has described the changes which turned the Constitution into the Treaty as "cosmetic changes", and the continued use of these Constitutional symbols proves her point.

It is an open question whether the parliament is in fact fifty years old. There was an appointed European assembly which first met in 1958, on the basis of which the celebration took place. But in fact the first elected parliament met in 1979, so it is now only 29 years old.

This shows the hypocrisy of the new Lisbon Treaty. The Government's promise on the EU flag and anthem has been proved completely hollow. Labour's decision to deny the people the referendum which they promised in its General Election Manifesto is a gross breach of faith. Whilst there is still time I urge Parliamentarians in Westminster to demand a referendum.

Of course, Tony Blair behaved disgracefully on this whole episode. He continued to claim that the Lisbon Treaty was something new, and railroaded it through Parliament. The only EU member state that did in fact hold a referendum on the Lisbon Treaty was Eire. This had nothing to do with any support for democracy on the part of the Irish government. If they could have avoided a referendum they would have done so, but the Irish constitution required that a referendum be held. It took place on 12 June 2008. The result was 53% No and 47% Yes.

The next day I wrote to the Irish Times.

Thank you Ireland

Dear Sir,

God bless the Irish! I thank you from the bottom of my heart, and on behalf of the eighty-percent-plus of my UK constituents who would have voted NO, but were denied their promised referendum.

Ireland has struck an historic blow for freedom and democracy, independence and self-determination. At last the cloth-eared Eurocrats in Brussels will have to listen to the people. Thank you, thank you, thank you.

Yours faithfully,

Roger Helmer MEP

Meanwhile a rumour swept through the EU zealots in Brussels that the Irish No campaign had been funded by a secret conclave of American neo-conservative billionaires. There were outraged squeaks from the EU apparatchiks condemning this apparent interference by the USA in the EU democratic process. The claims turned out to be utter nonsense, but many of those keenest on EU integration continued (and continue) to believe them. Anything rather than accept that the Irish did not like the Lisbon Treaty.

It was in this fevered atmosphere of imagined conspiracy theories and contempt for the great unwashed populace, that I got up at the Plenary Session in June to respond to a rather petulant and ill judged remark made by French President Sarkozy a few days earlier.

twitter
Leaving Brux passport control, I seem to be a 'Burger'. Do I come with fries?

Mr. President

President Sarkozy is reported in the London Times as saying: "The Irish are bloody fools. They have been stuffing their faces at Europe's expense for years, and now they dump us in the s**t". His word, not mine.

Last week we all said we respected the Irish result. But we do not respect it. We are treating the Irish with utter contempt. Like Robert Mugabe, we simply reject the verdict of the people.

Wolfgang Schaeuble says that a million Irish cannot decide for half a billion Europeans. Very well then. Let the half billion vote on the Treaty. You dare not, because you know they too would vote NO.

This very month the EU lost its last pretence of public consent or democratic legitimacy. You are revealed for what you are -- an authoritarian conspiracy against the people.

The referendum was in Ireland, but it was here in Brussels that democracy finally died. We are here today to bury it.

Things gradually calmed down a bit. In typical EU fashion, the élite then began moves to show their contempt for the public they ruled. You will recall that Tony Blair and others had pointed to the dropping of an EU anthem and EU flag as evidence that the Lisbon Treaty was different to the Constitution. In October the EU Parliament decided to adopt the flag and anthem anyway. I was incensed. I wrote on my website:

EU anthem in the parliament: we won't stand for it

MEPs have voted to play the EU anthem and adopt the official symbols of the union as part of a change in the parliament's rules today, but the idea has hit a low note with Conservative MEPs.

The parliament has backed proposals put forward by the top brass in the Constitutional Affairs committee. They would make the parliament recognise the EU flag, play Beethoven's 'Ode to Joy', celebrate Europe day and print the parliament's 'United in diversity' motto on all documents.

The inclusion of the symbols into the rules of procedure was originally part of the doomed EU Constitution but omitted from the Lisbon Treaty. This move is unnecessary, provocative and a waste of time and money.

Symbols and anthems are often used to promote nationhood, but many MEPs still do not understand that the people do not want to be part of a

European nation. The inclusion of the anthem and EU symbols in the parliament's functioning highlights the federalist intentions of a number of MEPs.

That was not the end of it. The EU powers that be were putting together a plan to enable them to ignore the democratic will of the people. The first move in the charade came on 11 December 2008 when Irish Taoiseach Brian Cowen went to Brussels and declared that the Irish voters had not really voted against Lisbon at all. Oh no. They had voted against EU policies on taxation, social affairs, ethical issues and military spending. Put that right, he said, and the Irish would vote the correct way. The European Council nodded their collective heads in wise agreement. Then they announced a series of "legal guarantees" on EU policies on taxation, social affairs, ethical issues and military spending.

These guarantees changed not a word of the Lisbon Treaty. The only real change came in the form of an unofficial understanding that Ireland could continue to appoint a Commissioner. Cowen then announced that all the concerns of the Irish people had been met and promised to hold another referendum.

That allowed the EU to move forward with ratification in those few countries that had not yet ratified the Lisbon Treaty. Among these were Britain and the Czech Republic. In Britain we were hoping that ratification could be delayed until after a General Election (due by

2010 at the latest) at which we hoped that Labour would be ousted and that an incoming Conservative government would hold the long promised referendum. Little did we know.

Meanwhile, the excellent Vaclav Klaus the Czech President, was holding out against ratification. He came under intense pressure from the EU institutions to drop his opposition. At the time much of this remained under wraps, but enough leaked out to prompt me to write an open letter to Hans-Gert Pöttering, President of the European Parliament, on 26th March 2009.

Dear Mr President

You are quoted by EU Observer as saying, with regard to possible delays in Czech ratification of the Lisbon Treaty, that "I cannot imagine that the Czech people, these 10 million people ... are going at the end of the day to stand against the 490 other million citizens of the European Union ... We have a historic responsibility to see this through".

This is an outrageous distortion of reality. You know perfectly well that the Treaty does not have the support of "490 million citizens across Europe". You know that if the Treaty were put to a referendum in the member-states it would fail in many of them, as it has already failed in Ireland. In the UK, opinion polls show 70%+ against the Treaty. President Sarkozy is reported as saying the Treaty would fail in France if put to the people.

The EU institutions are pressing ahead with Lisbon in defiance of public opinion. They are showing a monstrous contempt for the people and for democratic values, and they are widening the democratic deficit, the yawning gap between the ambitions of the EU élites, and the identity and aspirations of the citizens.

Say, if you will, that the Czech Republic is (or may be) standing against 26 other EU governments. But you cannot say that it is standing against 490 million people.

Regards

ROGER HELMER MEP

By this date the Irish referendum was beginning to attract attention. You will recall that those keen on EU integration and the Lisbon Treaty had cried "foul" when they had imagined (falsely) that US businessmen had poured money into the Irish No campaign. Well, in March things showed just how seriously those same people took Irish democracy. I explained my take on 19th March 2009:

EU Commission "to rig Irish referendum"

According to reports in the Irish press, the EU Commission is planning an "information" campaign designed to influence the outcome of the second Irish referendum on the Lisbon Treaty, expected this autumn. A meeting took place in Brussels on March 18th between the Commission and Mr. Martin Territt, head of the EU's representation in Dublin, to plan the campaign, which is expected to involve expenditure of around € 2 million.

Back in 2007 ahead of the first Irish referendum on Lisbon, a complaint was lodged by former Green MEP Patricia McKenna with the Irish Broadcasting Complaints Commission that the proposed EU Commission "information" campaign in Ireland was likely to influence (and clearly intended to influence) the outcome of the referendum. The complaint was upheld and the EU Commission's commercials were ruled to be political and therefore in breach of Irish broadcasting rules.

Now the Commission is trying again. I believe that the Commission's plan is an improper use of tax-payers' money, arguing that it is scandalous for the Commission to seek to influence the outcome of a referendum in this way. I believe that it is morally equivalent to the government of a member-state using public funds to campaign for the governing party in a general election. I have accordingly tabled a Written Question to the Commission, calling on them to abandon the plan.

It is scandalous enough that the EU institutions have rejected the democratic decision of the Irish people in the first referendum, and are demanding a second referendum -- although the EU repeatedly rejects NO votes and requires member-states to vote again. But to use tax-payers' money to influence the outcome is a disgrace. The EU is fundamentally anti-democratic, and examples like this prove the point.

They ignored me of course, but I had to speak out. The EU Parliament is a strange place. It often debates things that it does not need to talk about – apparently for no real reason other than that it gives MEPs the chance to sound off on a given subject and try to look good. The vast majority of MEPs are in favour of an EU superstate, and so they love to debate issues and matters that have to do with that subject. The Lisbon Treaty was a case in point. It cropped up again at the Plenary Session in May. And again – due my non inscrit status – I got to speak on the subject. I grabbed my chance with both hands:

Mr. President

I am sorry that Mr. Pöttering is not in the Chair tonight, as I had hoped to thank him publicly for giving me the opportunity to leave the EPP group a few years back. I am delighted that my Conservative colleagues will all be leaving the EPP shortly -- an objective I have worked towards for ten years.

We are here to debate the Lisbon Treaty, so I would also have reminded Mr. Pöttering that his own country, Germany, has not yet ratified.
We in the EU claim to be a Union of Values based on Democracy and the Rule of Law. Yet we ignore democracy. We ride roughshod over the wishes of

voters. We rejected the results of referenda in Denmark on Maastricht, in Ireland on Nice, in France & Holland on the Constitution, and now on Lisbon in Ireland again. We treat the aspirations of our electorates with outright contempt. So much for democracy.

We are no better on the Rule of Law. We are implementing plans and spending based on the Lisbon Treaty ahead of ratification. This is little less than a bloodless coup d'état.

Mr. Pöttering says that a million Irish voters cannot stand in the way of 450 million European citizens. He is right. So let the 450 million vote on the Treaty! Britain will vote No. In all probability France and Germany will vote No. But you dare not let the people vote, because you know the answer already.

In Britain, all but eight of our 646 MPs were elected on a commitment to a referendum, yet our discredited Labour government has scandalously broken its promise.

Let me give colleagues due notice. We in the British Conservative Party will make a Lisbon Referendum a key plank of our euro-election platform. We will deliver a referendum, and we will kill this shameful Treaty stone dead.

There then came the EU elections of June 2009. Once again I was honoured to have been put in No.1 position by the

ABOVE: In 2009 I was joined in Brussels by a new colleague as Conservative MEP for the East Midlands, Emma McClarkin. Here she is in her office on her first day in Brussels.

Conservative members in the East Midlands. The great East Midlands electorate voted to return two Conservative MEPs, plus one Labour, one LibDem and one UKIP MEP. My old friend Chris Heaton-Harris (who had been elected alongside me in 1999) chose to stand down to concentrate on his ambition to become an MP in Westminster. Chris was to be successful and as I write this in 2011 is now doing a sterling job as MP for Daventry. He was replaced as my Conservative MEP colleague by Emma McClarkin, now

working hard alongside me in Brussels.

Another change that took place at this time was that we Conservative MEPs finally left the EPP grouping. Instead we formed a new grouping called the European Conservative and Reformists (ECR). The group included a wide range of like-minded parties from other EU member states. The Guardian and other lefties made some carping criticisms from the sidelines, but the new grouping has proved to be a success. Freed from the EPP, we Conservatives have finally been able to employ our own researchers, vote as we wish and are generally free of that integrationist entity.

Back in the protracted struggle over the Lisbon Treaty things continued to grind on. In October 2009 Ireland voted

ABOVE: Immediately after the 2009 euro-elections, Conservative MEPs left the federalist EPP group (from which I had already been expelled) and helped to found the European Conservatives and Reformists group. Here I am pictured at a nuclear seminar, in front of our ECR logo, with fellow-Conservative MEP Giles Chichester (SouthWest Region).

again and this time they voted Yes to the Lisbon Treaty. Gordon Brown, by this date Prime Minister of Britain, hurried to ratify the treaty on behalf of Britain, as did the Germans and others. Even the Czechs caved in to pressure and they too ratified Lisbon.

Mr Cowen gathered the plaudits of the EU enthusiasts and basked in their approval. In 2010 he was to learn just how reliable his new friends were when the EU moved in to undermine the Irish economy and cynically threw him to the wolves. Mr Cowen is now out of a job. But I digress.

However, all was not yet lost. As noted in my speech of May given above, Conservative Party policy at this date was unequivocal: There would be a referendum on the Lisbon Treaty. In 2005 this policy had been a plank of the campaign by David Cameron in his successful bid to be Leader of the Conservative Party. In his own words it was a "cast iron guarantee". Along with his pledge to take the Conservative MEPs out of the pro-Lisbon and pro-integrationist EPP grouping, it had been this that persuaded me to back Mr Cameron as party leader. It had seemed a simple, clear and popular policy.

Then came the bombshell that the Conservative Party was ditching the policy. On 4 November David Cameron announced "The Lisbon treaty has now been ratified by every one of the 27 member states of the European Union, and our campaign for a referendum on the Lisbon treaty is therefore over. Why?" he asked himself rhetorically. "Because it is no longer a treaty: it is being incorporated into the law of the European Union. Next week, the new posts that the Lisbon treaty creates – a president and a foreign minister – will be filled. We cannot hold a referendum and magically make those posts – or the Lisbon treaty itself – disappear, any more than we could hold a referendum to stop the sun rising in the morning."

I was appalled, shocked and disappointed in equal measure. My response was swift and, for me personally, defining. I explained in an article published on the ConservativeHome website the next day.

Our new European policy is confused and essentially cosmetic – and I cannot defend it

Yesterday I joined a phone-in programme on the Lisbon Treaty on BBC Radio Northampton. I am well aware of public attitudes to the EU, yet even I was taken aback by the relentlessly hostile flow of comment about the Lisbon Treaty, and the way that it has been rail-roaded through in the teeth of public opposition. It is clear that the EU has lost any claim it might have had to democracy and legitimacy. Many speakers were also very unhappy about the withdrawal by the

Conservative Party of its commitment to a Lisbon referendum.

The presenter turned to me in the forlorn hope that, as an MEP in Brussels, I might have an alternative view. He was disappointed. Like all Conservative MPs and MEPs, I was elected on an explicit Manifesto Commitment to a referendum on the Lisbon Treaty. Yesterday, David Cameron rejected that commitment and repudiated that policy.

I respect the view of those who say that you can't have a referendum on a fully-ratified treaty, but I think they're wrong. Such a referendum would serve three ends: first we should be keeping our word. Second, we should put the spotlight on the shocking betrayal of the British people by this Labour government. But third, and most important, we should give a future Conservative government a rock-solid mandate for renegotiation.

Yet if those who argue against such a referendum win the day, we at least have an obligation to give the British people a say in some form. We have a clear duty to let the British people speak at last on this vexed issue.

Our new policy is confused. We have said that now that the Lisbon Treaty is EU law, we are not in a position to repudiate it. Yet we have made a series of proposals which repudiate significant parts of it, and run counter to EU law – – for example the proposed Sovereignty

Bill. But as we all know, the supremacy of EU Law is explicit in the Lisbon Treaty. If we accept Lisbon, we accept the supremacy of EU law.

A "Referendum Lock" will not work, because we have already thrown away the key. Our policy fails to recognise the self-amending nature of Lisbon, with its passerelle clauses. Until now, EU integration has been step-wise, Treaty by Treaty. Now it will become a continuous process of daily attrition, successive salami slices. That is, in large part, the main point of Lisbon. It is designed to eliminate the problems and referenda defeats which successive Treaties have faced, and to provide for integration by stealth. If we are not prepared to stand and fight on the enormity of the Treaty itself, we will scarcely stand and fight on the subsequent salami slices.

What we have is an essentially

BELOW: I went to Rutland in the course of the 2010 General Election campaign to help Alan Duncan, the sitting Conservative MP who was restanding. In Melton Mowbray I found our enthusiastic campaign team accompanied by this gorgeous dog with a very patriotic outfit.

cosmetic policy. We are installing a largely ineffective burglar alarm when the family silver has already been stolen. But the British people don't want vague promises. They want the family silver back in good order.

I intend to continue to support the Party, and to work for a Conservative victory in 2010, since it is over whelmingly in the best interests of my constituents, and of the country, to have a Conservative government under David Cameron, rather than the present failing and disastrous Labour administration.

But I can neither justify nor support our new EU policy. In these circumstances, I have concluded that I can no longer continue to serve as a spokesman for the delegation. I have accordingly resigned both my spokesmanships with immediate effect.

So have I given up in despair? Not yet. These developments are a set-back, but not yet a death-knell. For years I have publicly supported the Better Off Out campaign, and I will continue to do so. You can only defy the will of the people for so long, and the longer you do so the angrier they get. Transnational governments that fail to respect the identity and aspirations of the people cannot survive -- consider Yugoslavia, or the USSR.

We have lost the hope of a referendum on the Lisbon Treaty, but I believe that I shall live to see the day

when we have a referendum on EU membership, and Brussels is working hard, if unconsciously, to firm up the OUT vote. I put my faith in the angry callers of Northamptonshire, and others like them up and down the country.

This break marked a serious decline in my relations with David Cameron's Conservative hierarchy — though not I hasten to add with the ordinary members of the Conservative Party in the country and, in particular, in the East Midlands. My move was to have serious implications, but that tale is best told in a later chapter.

Meanwhile, the EU juggernaut ploughed on along its anti-democratic path toward the EU Project's dream of superstatehood. The fight in Brussels went on.

But it was not just that the EU superstate was anti-democratic in the theoretical area of constitutional niceties, important though this is. The bureaucratic monster that is the EU continued to have a malign impact on the everyday lives of people and businesses in the East Midlands. As MEP for the East Midlands it was, and remains, my job to represent my voters and to do battle with the EU behemoth.

A typical example surfaced in the spring of 2010 and prompted me to write on my website.

I am backing calls from balloonists

Ballooning enthusiasts are blighted with European legislation that negatively impacts on both recreational and commercial hot air ballooning. Following letters from several constituents, I have met with representatives from the British Balloon and Airship Club and neighbouring West Midlands Conservative MEP Philip Bradbourn to discuss the legislation.

Mr Bradbourn and I learnt how the European Aviation Safety Agency, which develops regulations for aircraft, is having a detrimental effect on ballooning by dramatically increasing bureaucracy. It used to take one hour, including form-filling, to inspect a hot air balloon whereas now it takes several hours. Due to the volume of paperwork the British Balloon and Airship Club has now had to start charging balloonists £100 + VAT for an inspection on top of the hourly rate for the inspectors. With the inspection fee and the increased length of time for an inspection it is estimated that hundreds of balloons throughout the UK are grounded as owners cannot afford to comply with the EU regulations.

It is not commonly known but the UK is the largest manufacturer of hot air balloons in the world, estimated to be worth around £10m per annum. Mr Bradbourn and I were extremely concerned to hear the representatives' anxieties that if both private enthusiasts and those who fly hot air balloons commercially cannot afford to keep their balloons manufacturing will also decline.

Mr Ian Warrington, a hot air balloon pilot based in Rutland, told us: "The European Aviation Safety Agency has a broad and unrefined approach. If the demands and costs resulting from the European red tape continue to increase many private pilots will simply give up."

This one-size-fits-all approach of the European legislation which groups together hot air balloons with jumbo jets is simply not practical. The leisure and commercial sector of ballooning, and also gliding, were extremely effective and safe when they were self-regulated. The European regulations do not raise safety standards, just add costs and unnecessary paperwork. My Conservative colleagues and I will seek action from the European Commission to exclude gliding and ballooning from these unnecessary regulations which only interfere in a pastime that should be pleasurable and fun.

Other constituency duties kept me busy now that I was freed from my spokesmanship duties. On 30 April 2010 I went to Uppingham School to speak in a debate on the EU. I blogged about the experience next day.

Cambridge beats Oxford in Uppingham

Last night, April 30th, I was privileged to speak in a debate at Uppingham School, in the County of Rutland, against a motion in favour of "Ever Closer Union". Uppingham, by the

way, has magnificent buildings. You could film Harry Potter there. I could not help contrasting it with my own old school, King Edward VI Southampton, which while equally venerable (1554), has buildings from the mid 20th Century and looks like a biscuit factory.

My opponent was Oxford academic and former journalist Dr. Graham Jones, who seems to be the European Movement's point man for the East Midlands. The event, organised by politics teacher Toby Makhzangi, took place in the lecture theatre and was attended by 20+ pupils (we were up against a General Election hustings meeting elsewhere in the school, with local MP Alan Duncan, with whom I shall be campaigning this afternoon). I was introduced by a pupil, Amy.

ABOVE: The EU Parliament hosts a wide range of informal meetings on a wide range of subjects. Many of these are worthy occasions (though at times a bit dull), but every now and then a speaker will make a surprising remark that catches us all by surprise. As can be seen from the reactions at this event, this was one such.

It was a lively and (I thought) interesting debate – quite combative at times, especially when my opponent, a self-confessed Lib-Dem, started reciting the standard Guardian agit-prop about our Polish allies in the European parliament.

My own take on the debate was that Cambridge beat Oxford by a clear margin. But then I would think that, wouldn't I?

31

Still the nonsense continued to spew out of the Brussels machine. And with little by way of democratic check on them, they became ever more ridiculous. Take, for instance, the threat to the British habit of purchasing a dozen eggs rather than a pound — sorry demi kilogramme — of eggs. I explained on my website.

EU attempts to ban a dozen eggs

New legislation being considered by the EU would block shops from selling food by quantity and restrict them to sell by weight only. The move, if implemented, would see a dozen eggs become a thing of the past.

The proposal will be fought at the European Council as the UK's food law does allow the labelling of pre-packed foods by number. When the proposed law to only allow food to be sold by weight reaches the European Parliament MEPs will then have the opportunity to scrap this legislation.

First they tried to ban pounds and ounces, then bendy fruit and veg, and now some within the EU have turned to attacking groceries labelled by number. This plan would mean that each egg box would have to be weighed individually, adding costs to producers who would then pass it on to the consumer. It would also bring unnecessary confusion to shoppers who have always bought eggs by number.

My colleague as a Conservative MEP for the East Midlands, Emma McClarkin had the best line on this. "It is little wonder that people are cracking up with the EU when it comes forward with laws such as this," she said.

On 1 July the new ECR Group to which we Conservative MEPs belong had as a guest speaker the then new semi-permanent President of the EU Council to address us. Mr. Herman Van Rompuy is a Belgian national and former (temporary) Belgian Prime Minister (he seems to specialise in temporary rôles — perhaps a Belgian trait). His name, however, is very difficult for Anglo-Saxon tongues to cope with, so I'm happy to think of him as Rumpy Pumpy. He is, of course the man famously (if perhaps unkindly) described by Nigel Farage as "having all the charisma of a damp rag".

The ECR was celebrating the appointment of Petr Necas, the leader of the Civic Democrat/ODS Party (part of the ECR) in the Czech Republic, as Prime Minister. The appointment meant that ECR parties now held the premiership in two EU member-states — the UK and the Czech Republic.

I had the opportunity to put a question to Rumpy Pumpy, and I managed to slip in the old hoary chestnut about the advice we should give to the US President if he wished to talk to the EU President, of whom there seem to be four at the last count. José Manuel Barroso is President of the Commission. Jerzy Buzek is President of the European Parliament. Then there is Rumpy Pumpy, as President of the Council. But of course we still retain, for the moment, the EU's farcical six-month rotating Presidency, which is due to fall to Belgium tomorrow, July 1st. But as Belgium is currently lacking a government – as seems so often the case – it is quite difficult to put a name to its rotating President. And if we don't know, how is the State Department supposed to work it out?

Rumpy Pumpy assured us that the lines of responsibility were crystal clear, and that the 600 pages of the Lisbon Treaty had made them even clearer. Forgive the tired cliché, but the phrase "clear as mud" springs to mind. But my substantive question went more or less as follows:

> "Mr. President, there is a series of opinion polls which seems to show that the EU is rapidly losing the support of citizens. The Greeks are out on the streets protesting against what they see as EU austerity policies, while the Germans are furious at having to bail out the Greeks, and the prospect of bank-rolling other Club Med states too. Meantime a poll published only today shows that a majority of Germans would like their Deutschmark back, and only 30% approve of the euro. We know that in the UK, if we had had the promised referendum on the Lisbon Treaty, it would have been overwhelmingly rejected.
>
> "I know that the Commission has given some thought to ways in which it might bring public opinion more closely into line with EU policies and

twitter

Barosso: "Government legitimacy depends on listening to the people". So why does the EU ignore referendum results?

> objectives. I wonder if you, Mr. President, would consider re-framing the question, and think about ways to bring EU policies more closely into line with the objectives and aspirations of the citizens?"

And answer came there none.

Looking back, I realise that it was on this same day that I had one of my more bizarre experiences in the Parliament. At the time I referred to it as "My Kafka Day in Brussels". The event was prompted by the decision of the powers that be that the Parliament's Visitor Centre was to have a new video installation. On this video wall was to be played an endless loop of video consisting of each and every MEP making a short statement. Why this was thought to be a good idea is beyond me, but never mind. I trotted off to record my piece.

The invitation I had received said that the statement would be recorded in Room JAN -1 Q100. The labyrinth that is the EU Parliament is made up of several different buildings, each of which has a name that is habitually truncated to a three letter code – in this case JAN. The floor is then indicated by the first number. In this case -1 meant the first floor in the basement. In typical EU fashion, the room numbering system within each building is different. It can cause confusion. It did now. I blogged what happened next.

When I got to Floor Minus One in the new JAN Building, it was like the Marie Celeste, or a Kafka novel. Long deserted corridors, locked doors on either side, and not a single soul in evidence. To all appearances, vast sums of tax-payers' money spent to little purpose. I wandered back and forth for some time with no sign of Room Q100, nor any Q rooms for that matter.

Eventually, I found three guys walking down a corridor, and asked them for directions. It turned out they had come to meet me, so we finally found the studio, and I was recorded against a plain green background (to allow them to put in the EU flag afterwards, I guess!). After eleven years in politics, I wasn't expecting new experiences, but for the first time I was able to use a tele-prompt. I had prepared a few words for my 45-second statement, and one of the guys typed it into their system — I don't know what he made of it. If I'd been advised in advance, I could have e-mailed it and saved him the trouble.

Here's the text:

"I'm Roger Helmer, and I'm a British Conservative MEP representing the East Midlands Region. I decided to stand for the European parliament in 1999 because I was profoundly unhappy at the way the EU was going.

"I support trade and cooperation in Europe, but I am opposed to the creation of supra-national political structures which are undemocratic, unresponsive and unaccountable, and which treat the views of citizens with contempt. In repeated referendums, the EU has ignored the verdict of the people.

"I believe that the EU is making us poorer, and less democratic, and less free. We need a looser and more flexible Europe based on trade and cooperation."

I expected this little contribution to be conveniently lost in the editing process. To my amazement, however, it made it through and features on the video wall at the visitor centre. If you ever find yourself in the visitor centre and find that your feet stray to the video wall I would advise you not to linger in hope of seeing my few words. There are hundreds upon hundreds of MEPs, and that is a lot of talking heads to watch. On the other hand if you are having trouble sleeping it might cure you.

One of the ongoing disputes in the EU is the status of Turkey. Officially Turkey is welcome to join the EU just as soon as some minor details are ironed out. In fact, the EU is desperate to keep Turkey out and so a succession of details is invented to achieve this. Conservative Party policy is to welcome Turkey. I have never been entirely certain that is correct. In July 2010 David Cameron went to Ankara, which is in the Asian part of Turkey, to reiterate this policy.

I gave my response on my blog as follows:

David Cameron in Ankara has said that "prejudice" is blocking Turkish accession to the EU. That's the kind of cheap shot we'd expect from a Labour politician discussing immigration, not from a Conservative Prime Minister. He should pause and reflect that opponents of Turkish accession may have perfectly logical policy reasons for their opposition – as I do.

It's worth reviewing some of the arguments used by Cameron and others on this issue.

"As a staunch member of NATO, Turkey should be rewarded with EU membership". The USA is also a staunch member of NATO, but no one is suggesting it should join the EU. So is Norway, but it understands it is better off outside the EU. We should not be trading political union in exchange for military alliance.

"Turkey is an important trading partner with a growing economy". True. So are China and India (I applaud Cameron's initiative in India), but we're not inviting them to join the EU. Turkey already has access to the Single Market, and has been offered a "privileged partnership". Indeed I once spoke in the Strasbourg plenary on this, pointing out that a privileged partnership offered most of the benefits of membership with few of the costs, so was actually better than full membership

– and I got a shock/horror reaction when I argued that such a relationship would be better for the UK too!

"Turkey in the EU would demonstrate that a moderate Islamic country can co-exist with Western values". Maybe. I admire Turkey's secular tradition. But the Turkish government is already struggling to keep the lid on Islamism. We might allow a secular Turkey to accede to the EU, only to find a few years later that we had a fundamentalist cuckoo in the nest.

"Turkey is a populous country with a young demographic – just the thing to off-set aging Western populations". True. Turkey has a larger population than any EU country except Germany, and on current trends will overtake Germany within twenty years. If it joined the EU, it would expect the largest voting share. And here is the fundamental objection to Turkish membership: each new member-state dilutes what remains of our democracy and independence, and a very large state like Turkey dilutes it massively. I don't see why Turkey should have a bigger say in making laws that affect us here in the UK than we Brits have.

But this raises another issue: immigration. It has now become respectable to speak about immigration, without Labour leaders shouting "Racist!" (which is why it is so disappointing to hear Cameron trotting out the "prejudice" card). At the last election, worries about immigration, not entirely unjustified, were a top issue on the doorstep. It is really extraordinary that we should be proposing to open the floodgates (are we allowed to say "floodgates"? I will anyway) to potentially millions of people from a very different and relatively poor country. In Germany there is a large Turkish population; in France there is a large North African population; and these groups have given rise to serious social problems and tensions. To say that is not to apportion blame; still less to demonstrate prejudice. It is simply a statement of fact, and no British government will be forgiven if it invites similar problems here. It would be lunacy to offer free movement to Turkey, not least because Turkey's own borders are not secure from the east.

France & Germany have taken a much more rational approach to the issue, and though I hate to say it, this time Sarkozy and Merkel are right, and Cameron is wrong. Several continental countries have guaranteed their people a referendum on Turkish accession, and it is inconceivable that it would be approved. Indeed a cynic might conclude that Cameron was scoring cheap brownie points in Ankara by talking up Turkish accession, secure in the knowledge that he would never have to pick up the tab.

I suspect that any referendum on Turkish accession would be lost in the UK too. Certainly I find ordinary Conservative Party members bewildered by the Leadership's obsession with

Turkey, and almost universally opposed to Turkey in the EU.

Personally I should like to see more emphasis on the Anglosphere (Cameron's India mission is an excellent start) and less on an EU whose centre of gravity is moving eastwards.

But let me offer an olive branch to Cameron and Hague: if they can reduce the EU to what it should be – a simple Free Trade Area – then I will lead the charge for Turkish accession. And Israel. And Taiwan. But not while the EU is a political union.

So in my view, if Turkey joins the EU, then the UK would be Better Off Out. Indeed come to think of it, the UK would be Better Off Out anyway.

Now by this date I had grown so sceptical about the EU and all its works that I thought nothing they could do would take me by surprise. I realised with some surprise on 5th September 2010 that I was wrong when we MEPs received a quite remarkable email from the office of the President of the EU Commission (no less) José Manuel Barroso. I was so astonished that I at once turned to my internet connection and blogged on the issue.

Barroso No-Mates tries to buy a few pals

We have got the news that the parliament's "Conference of Presidents" (Presidents are two-a-penny in the EU) has taken the extraordinary step of proposing to dock the expenses of any MEP who fails to attend Barroso's big "State of the Union" speech on Tuesday in Strasbourg.

Imagine, if you will, Congress in Washington deciding it had to offer some kind of financial incentive to ensure Congressmen showing up to hear the real President's State of the Union address, and you will see the absurdity immediately. This move is demeaning to the parliament and to MEPs, as though they were incapable of organising their time. It is still more demeaning to Barroso, since it is a confession that MEPs might have better things to do than to listen to his vapourings. I suspect that Barroso's staff are furious at this publicity own-goal.

Now, it emerges, Barroso is planning to pay journalists' expenses to accompany him on foreign trips to "raise his profile". He is concerned that they don't write enough about the EU and its Commission President. They don't, but that's for the excellent reason that their readers are not very interested in the EU and its doings, and a Barroso headline doesn't sell papers.

This is in addition to the £6.6 million the EU has spent on "training" and "informing" journalists in the last year (with special emphasis on the Irish referendum). The Commission calls all this "communication", by which they mean propaganda. For the Commission, communication isn't phone bills. It's Agitprop.

Apparently this is also in large part about the EU's internal politics. Afraid of being upstaged by the President of the Council, Rumpy Pumpy, or even (some hope) by the self-effacing "Foreign Minister" Baroness Ashton, Barroso wants to build his personal profile. Looks like a big job.

I'm really not sure what to do on Tuesday. Check in and walk out? Stay but don't press the button? I'm sure there will be one or two points of order made. Admittedly they're talking a penalty for not attending, rather than an incentive to attend. But whichever way you approach it, it gets to look more and more like Thirty Pieces of Silver.

The press across the EU in general – not just in Britain for a once – was brutally hostile to this move. Just two days later we got another email from the office of the Commission President (two in one week, I was amazed). Again, I blogged at once:

An embarrassing climb-down in Strasbourg

I blogged recently about the parliament's extraordinary decision to offer MEPs a financial inducement (or rather a penalty for absence) to attend Commission President Barroso's "State of the Union" address this morning in Strasbourg. They were treating MEPs rather like hired extras in a film set — there to make up a crowd scene.

The parliament's "Conference of Presidents" was taken aback by the huge wave of contempt and derision that greeted their decision. Someone described it as "like a meeting of Brezhnev's Soviet Duma" (only there the penalty was a life-time in Siberia). And not only from the usual suspects. Even that Goody-Two-Shoes europhile the Lib-Dem MEP Sarah (Baroness) Ludford was on record with her opposition. So at least they have had the good grace to climb down and withdraw the threat.

After the meeting I blogged again.

Barroso's speech was a wonderfully rich tapestry of cliché and wishful thinking. Growth. Jobs. Progress. Economic renewal. Financial regulation. Freedom, Justice and Security. Competitiveness in the face of globalisation. European defence and security. A European Foreign Service. And an initiative to cut € 38 billion from the cost of red-tape (don't hold your breath!). As many speakers pointed out, this was about Barroso's vision for the future, and very little to do with the State of the Union as it is today.

Then Joseph Daul, leader of the EPP Group, spoke. His constant theme was "The citizens are calling for more Europe!" (I don't know which of the citizens he's been speaking to — not one of my 4.2 million constituents has ever told me they want "More Europe"!). It was only last year that we

Conservatives left the EPP, and I was thinking about how we might feel about Daul's speech if we were still in the EPP's maw.

The best speech came from Nigel Farage (UKIP leader). While the "State of the Union" title was a clear attempt to ape the USA, Farage pointed out a key difference between Barroso and a US President — US presidents are elected by the people. And (argued Farage) the true state of the union is shown in the Commission's own EU Barometer study, which demonstrates that confidence in the EU and its institutions has dropped dramatically over the last year, and that only 42% of citizens now regard membership of the EU as a good thing.

Meanwhile, my good colleague and a Conservative MEP Dan Hannan, who represents the South East Region of England, had launched a campaign for a referendum in Britain. Dan was not calling for a referendum on the despised, but by this date fully implemented, Lisbon Treaty. He had greater ambitions. He wanted a referendum on whether Britain should leave the EU altogether.

Dan's EU Referendum Campaign (EURC) is a cross-party initiative calling for the public to have a say on whether Britain is governed from Westminster or Brussels. So far as Dan and I were concerned the EU is making us poorer, and less democratic, and less free. The EU is costing Britain up to £120 billion a year, including regulatory costs – and it was set to rise as Brussels demanded an

38

end to the UK rebate.

I was happy to join Dan's initiative and at the time issued a press release in which I stated:

> In my experience people are fed up with the EU. The EU's own Eurobarometer survey shows only 42% of EU citizens believe that EU membership is good for them. It is preposterous that our government is discussing a referendum on PR, which no one much wants, instead of an EU referendum which all parties promised and which many people want passionately.

The brand new EURC organisation has its base in Westminster and is made up of a team of experienced campaigners who want to highlight that the British people still haven't had their promised referendum.

Now is the time to act, they say, as the government seeks an electoral reform through a referendum in 2011 which could, according to the EURC,

BELOW: The Bruges Group is an excellent organisation promoting a more sensible vision for the future of the EU. At their fringe meeting at the 2010 Conservative Party Conference, I was proud to share a platform with the Daily Mail's forthright Melanie Philips.

twitter

Another "Citizen's Agora". The European Parliament continues to push post-democratic "governance by NGOs."

cost the country up to £80 million. Instead of such time-wasting exercises, efforts should instead be ploughed into providing a referendum for more important issues, such as who governs Britain.

They argue that the longer Britain relinquishes power to Brussels, the more difficult it will be to walk away from the emerging super-state. They are calling for voters to sign the petition for a referendum, which can be found at www.eureferendumcampaign.com

Dan may have got my support, but Don did not. The Don in question was Don Foster, MP for Bath. Now Bath is not in my East Midlands Region of England and while it is a lovely town, I had never heard of Don Foster MP (he had probably not heard of me either, so fair enough). On 26 September I was listening to the BBC Radio 4 Ten O'Clock News, when I heard a contribution from this Don Foster MP. I assumed he might be a Conservative because he was up against Nigel Farage of UKIP. I was alarmed by his comments on Britain's EU membership. And I was only partly mollified later to find that he is in fact the Lib-Dem Member for Bath. In the context, he was speaking (or would be taken to be

speaking) for the Coalition, and therefore, by extension, for me.

"Damn cheek", I thought. I turned to my blog and made my protest:

Don Foster asserted that the net cost of Britain's EU membership is "only" around £4 billion, and that this "was good value for all we get in exchange". This is just plain wrong on so many levels that it's difficult to know where to start.

For a start, even our net contribution to the EU budget is well over £4 billion, and set to increase rapidly as a result of Tony Blair's ill-advised deal on the rebate. Secondly, as my colleague Dan Hannan has cogently argued, we don't think of our income tax in net terms (after all the benefits we get back from government) — we think of what we have to pay. The funds we get back from the EU are hedged about with restrictions, often require matched funding, and are often spent inefficiently on things we might not have chosen to do. The EU gives us back a little of our own money, they tell us what to do with it, and they expect us to be grateful. On a gross basis our contribution is around £13 billion, and rapidly escalating.

But the direct contributions to the EU Budget are not the half of it. The greatest cost by far of our EU membership is the huge and unsustainable burden of regulation, which is strangling our economy, and (despite assurances to the contrary) getting worse by the day. Various analyses of regulatory costs have been prepared, not least by Commissioner Verheugen, who estimated the cost of regulation at around 5.5% of GDP (compared to the benefits of trade in the Single Market, estimated at 1.8%). The British Chambers of Commerce have done extensive analyses. One of the most credible estimates of the total net costs of Britain's EU membership, from the Taxpayers' Alliance, puts it at well over £100 billion a year.

Then Mr. Foster talks of "the benefits of EU membership", which we get in exchange for this vast expenditure. I've said it so many times before, but it can't be said too often: There are no benefits of EU membership that could not be obtained through a simple Free Trade Agreement. We could have the benefits without the huge costs to our economy and our democracy and independence.

No doubt Mr. Foster will disagree with me, but in that case I hope that he will at least support the demand, from myself and others, for a White Paper on costs and benefits of Britain's EU membership. Previous governments have refused on the grounds that "the benefits are self-evident". Yet when the Swiss government undertook a very thorough and professional analysis of the costs and benefits of Switzerland's proposed membership of the EU, the answer was that the costs overwhelmingly outweighed the benefits. Switzerland concluded that it was Better Off Out. And so should we be.

As chance would have it one of my constituents had also heard the radio piece and was just as annoyed as was I. He wrote to Foreign Secretary William Hague asking a string of questions and got in reply what was obviously a standardised missive from an official that failed to answer his points. None too impressed, he passed copies of his correspondence on to me. I was equally unimpressed and wrote to the Foreign Office as follows:

Mr. John Brunskill,
Europe Directorate,
Foreign & Commonwealth Office

Dear John,

I have a copy of what appears to be a standard letter from you to a member of public concerned about European issues, and I have to say that I am extremely disappointed that a letter written by a great department of state during a Conservative-led administration should be so biased in favour of the EU, and so out-of-touch with public opinion.

You were responding to a letter which asked specifically why British Conservative MEPs had been whipped to vote in support of the European External Action Service (EEAS) in Strasbourg in July. You made no attempt to answer this point at all. I appreciate that it is not your job to take a political position, but the original enquiry was addressed to William Hague (to whom we might expect to look for a political response), and his office referred it to you for a reply. Instead, the enquirer got an anodyne standard letter which might well have been — probably was — drafted under the previous Labour administration.

May I respond to a number of your points.

"The Government believes that membership of the EU is in the national interest". Why? And why then will the Government not commission a cost/benefit analysis of EU membership which would settle this question once and for all? You will be aware that when Switzerland did such an analysis, the answer was resoundingly negative.

"The Government ... is confident of the UK's ability to move the EU in the right direction". Surely the triumph of hope over experience. The UK has now been a member of the EU for nearly forty years, and has failed under either Labour or Conservative administrations to change its direction. Moves to "ever closer union" continue apace.

"The Government has agreed that there should be no further transfer of sovereignty during the life of this parliament". But it has been transferring sovereignty rapidly in its first few months. It has supported the EEAS (the subject of the original enquiry to which your letter fails to respond); it has accepted the European Investigation Order, without the safeguards that other member-states

have insisted on; it has rolled over without a fight on EU financial regulation.

"Any future Treaty ... will be subject to a Referendum Lock". But the Lisbon Treaty contains passerelle clauses which obviate the need for any new treaty. The EU can pursue further integration measures without any new treaty. The "Referendum Lock" shuts the stable door after the horse has bolted.

In response to a query on the costs of EU membership, you simply quote the Treasury figures for net budget contributions. Why net? On that basis you could say that taxation in the UK is negative, on the grounds that the government spends more than it collects. But the direct budget contributions, as you well know (or ought to know) are only a fraction of the total cost of membership, estimated by commentators like the Tax Payers' Alliance at £120 billion a year, when you include regulatory and other costs. I hesitate to use the term "deceitful", but it is at least deeply misleading to quote only net EU budget contributions.

"In return ... we get better access for British companies to EU markets .... 3.5 million jobs are linked ... to trade with the EU". It is not clear that we get better market access than would be available with a simple Free Trade Agreement (such as many other countries have with the EU), and such an agreement would avoid the crippling costs of membership (both the money

costs and the costs in terms of democratic accountability). The National Institute for Economic & Social Research, which originated your 3.5 million jobs figure, has been appalled by the way it has been misinterpreted. It may be that those jobs depend on the trade, but they do not depend on the EU membership. If it is true that 3.5 million UK jobs depend on trade with the EU, it is certainly true that many more EU jobs depend on trade with the UK. There is no reason to believe that there would be fewer jobs under a simple FTA.

You insist that (the British) Parliament is sovereign – yet it dare not exercise that sovereignty, and meantime probably three-quarters of our new laws come from unaccountable foreign institutions in Brussels, with no more than the most derisory scrutiny in Westminster.

It is time for the establishment — and the FCO — to wake up to what the British public understand: that EU membership is making us poorer, and less democratic, and less free. Your letter is profoundly misleading and complacent, and it is time for a wake-up call.

Yours sincerely,

ROGER HELMER MEP

As I mentioned in this letter, one of the recurrent problems that blight Britain's relationship with the EU is money. In particular the size of the EU budget is a thorny issue that comes up periodically. Since Gordon Brown and Tony Blair signed away the bulk of the budget rebate won by Margaret Thatcher, that problem has become increasingly important. As incoming Prime Minister of Britain, David Cameron had to face up to the issue sooner or later. At the end of October 2010 he ventured out to Brussels to tackle the subject. On 3rd November I blogged my thoughts.

The EU Budget, now that the dust has settled

Last week, David Cameron went to Brussels to negotiate the EU Budget. Now that the dust has settled, it's time to consider how he got on.

Before he went, he was very clear. The EU budget should be cut, just as national budgets were being cut, or at least frozen. Many of us were rather surprised, therefore, when he came back to announce a great British success: the budget was to be raised by "only" 2.9%. But this was exactly the position previously agreed by the Council in August, so on the face of it, it was no success at all — merely the Council's status quo. Cameron was forced to argue that the Council had at least firmed up its negotiating position.

His announcement had echoes of John Major's notorious "Game, Set & Match" sound-bite after Maastricht, or even Chamberlain's infamous "Peace in our time" claim after Munich in 1938.

ABOVE: I was delighted to join Dan Hannan, a Conservative MEP for the South East Region of England, in calling on the Labour government to hold a referendum on the Lisbon Treaty. I sponsored the advan and managed to get it parked outside the Houses of Parliament for just long enough to get a number of photos taken.

We need to understand that even now, the Council's position is only an opening negotiating stance. There will now be horse-trading between the Council, the parliament and the Commission, and seasoned Brussels-watchers will be surprised if the outcome is not somewhere north of 2.9%.

Even at 2.9%, we will be giving nearly an extra half billion pounds a year to Brussels. And that's on top of the extra two or three billion we are handing over as a result of Tony Blair's hopelessly inept negotiations several years ago, when he gave away a large part of Maggie Thatcher's Fontainebleau rebate, in exchange for nebulous promises about CAP reform.

Now, however, we have a new element in the mix. Germany's Chancellor Angela Merkel wants a tougher sanctions régime for eurozone states that run up excessive deficits, as Greece has done. This will require a change in the Treaties, although it is not totally clear at this stage whether it actually needs an entirely new Treaty (the EU is desperate to avoid any further referenda, which it would expect to lose), or whether they can make use of the Lisbon Treaty's "passerelle clauses" to alter the existing Treaty.

But either way (I understand), the UK will have a veto, and if it's a new Treaty, a pretext for a referendum. Just now, eurosceptic Tories (the overwhelming majority of the Party's members and activists) are increasingly disillusioned with the new Conservative-led government's approach to Brussels. We have rolled over on the EU diplomatic service, on EU financial regulation, on the European Investigation Order — and even on "Votes for Convicts". Our government has shown a spectacular lack of backbone.

But now we face a litmus test. Does Cameron have a shopping list? Will he use his potential veto to make serious demands of Brussels, and to start repatriating powers (he could start with the Working Time Directive, and employment law generally)? Or will he let another opportunity slip by? Unless he makes a stand, more and more Party members will start to wonder why they work their socks off for a Party that so spectacularly fails to deliver on this touchstone issue.

I was not greatly surprised, but disappointed nonetheless, to watch as David Cameron missed his chance.

Once again a British Prime Minister behaved as if the EU were his master.

One British Prime Minister who had no truck with the concept of Britain being ruled by a undemocratic foreign institution was Winston Churchill. As Churchill put it, "Democracy is the worst form of government we know — apart from all the others". But that message doesn't seem to have got through to the EU.

A year or two ago, the parliament organised a couple of "Agoras". That's a pretentious word for a Conference. The topics were European integration, and climate change. I attended both, and was more or less the only dissenter at each. Another was held in January 2011. I decided to blog on the subject as follows:

Of course the EU craves democratic legitimacy, and the European parliament exists primarily to give an impression (the word "fig-leaf" springs to mind) of democratic legitimacy to institutions which are palpably corporatist and technocratic, and fundamentally unaccountable and undemocratic, if not actually anti-democratic. At these Agoras, the idea was openly canvassed that "Representative democracy has failed, so we must move on to a new model of participative democracy".

twitter

"EU membership is in our national interest" says Europe Minister David Lidington. The hell it is! http://is.gd/hu5kS

This begs two questions. First, why or how has representative democracy failed? And second, what on earth do they mean by "participative democracy"?

The EU perceives two key ways in which representative democracy has failed. First, the voters in their ignorance, and with their prejudices, are prepared to elect to the European parliament MEPs who are fundamentally at odds with the whole EU project — MEPs like myself, or Dan Hannan, or Nigel Farage. Secondly, on most (not quite all) occasions when the public are invited in referenda to vote on EU questions, they give the wrong answer. So they have to vote again, or they are presented with the same proposition in a different wrapper (the EU Constitution/Lisbon Treaty), and told they can't have a referendum the second time. The EU simply can't work if the public are allowed a say, so clearly we have to get away from representative democracy.

And "participative democracy"? Why, that means consulting with civil society. And what's civil society? I remember at one of these events, causing outrage by saying that I did not know what civil society was. "I know who the people are", quoth I, "they vote for me, and I represent them. But I don't know what you mean by civil society". But now I do, and it's simple. They mean NGOs – Non Governmental Organisations.

The EU assembles the leaders of NGOs and quangoes, and consults with them. And the scandal is that for the most part, the EU funds them as well. In a very real sense, they're simply paying people to tell them what they want to hear.

And what right do the leaders of these NGOs have to claim to be representative, or claim to have democratic legitimacy? OK, maybe the RSPB has two million members, but they're mostly kindly folk who want to protect birds, and may have no interest in ruining the economy or threatening Europe's energy security with the extreme green measures that the EU and the NGOs discuss. People who find their way to leadership positions in these organisations are frequently single-issue zealots with no claim to any kind of broad mandate.

The other point is this: these people tend to be very comfortable indeed with the corporatist ethos of the EU, which results in a very agreeable and cosy dialogue. No wonder EU apparatchiks like to deal with these folk, rather than the great unwashed public. I can't help recalling that a similar model of pseudo-democratic governance was attempted in Italy in the 1930s. It was called fascism, and its chief exponent was Mussolini.

Dan Hannan says that the EU is making us poorer, and less democratic, and less free. Of course he's right, and this move to post-democratic governance illustrates the process.

The EU is set on its course. When I came to Brussels in 1999 I thought that the EU could be reformed. I thought that Britain could lead that movement. I thought we could make the EU better. Now I know that I was wrong.

Now I know that Britain would be Better Off Out.

ABOVE: In April 2010 I visited the Rushcliffe on Soar power station, just outside Nottingham, which is familiar to anyone who travels up and down the M1. Energy security is a terribly important policy area that was shamefully neglected by the Labour government in their rush to embrace the bunny-hugger vote.

A Sceptic on the Euro

The more astute among you will have noticed that in the opening chapter on the EU I failed to mention the Euro. This currency has had a turbulent history just recently, so I thought it deserved a chapter to itself.

The Euro predated my arrival in Brussels. The idea goes way back, but it was crystalised in 1992 in the Maastricht Treaty – though it was then termed the European Currency Unit or Ecu. The name of Euro was adopted in 1995 after it was realised that the French – cunning chaps that they are – had pulled a blinder. The Ecu was a little known traditional French currency unit that had predated the rather better known Franc.

The Maastricht Treaty made it compulsory for most EU member states to adopt the Euro as their currency if and when they met certain criteria. Denmark and Britain were not included in this obligation – John Major's famous "opt out" – though they are free to join the Euro if they wish to do so.

By the time I arrived in Brussels in 1999, most EU member states had permanently fixed their exchange rates,

the first step to adopting the currency. In 2002 the Euro replaced the national currencies in Austria, Belgium, Holland, Finland, France, Germany, Eire, Italy, Luxembourg, Portugal, Spain and Greece. They were followed by Slovenia in 2007, by Malta, Slovakia and Cyprus in 2008, and by Estonia in 2011.

Sweden, having first agreed to join the Euro, then managed to avoid doing so by deliberately failing to meet the entrance criteria. A few countries outside the EU had also adopted the Euro. These are tiny states such as Monaco, the Vatican, Andorra and San Marino. Bosnia and Herzegovina had not adopted the Euro, but had pegged their currency to it.

By 2007 when I finally realised that Britain would be Better Off Out of the EU, the Euro was being acclaimed a huge success by the Euro élite. It had become the second largest reserve currency in the world, was the second most traded currency and had the highest combined value (in terms of notes and coins) of any currency. In the first two points the Euro was second only to the US dollar – a fact which caused much gnashing of teeth among the EU zealots due to their institutionalised anti-Americanism.

From the day of its introduction as a cash currency, the Euro had steadily gained in value against the US Dollar, the Japanese Yen and the Swiss Franc. It gave every appearance of being a stable and effective currency, and was loudly praised as such by pretty much everyone I met in Brussels during those years.

---
twitter

William Hague on Today: "I know Roger Helmer. He'll not be happy till we have a government that will take us out of the EU". Indeed!

Predictably those most enthusiastic about the Euro were those most enthusiastic about the EU superstate. The currency was not and never had been an economic project. It was a political project from Day One. It was seen as one more step – and an important one at that – on the way towards the political unification of the continent.

I will not rehearse here the reasons why Britain has been right to stay out of this political experiment. Suffice it to say that our economy is different in some fundamental ways from those of most states within the Euro and that this means that we have rather different demands on our currency than do they. Those arguments have been made by others much better than I could hope to do, most notably by my colleague Dan Hannan. The control of monetary policy is an essential precondition of national sovereignty.

What amused and annoyed me in equal measure was the way that those in favour of the Euro as a political project so often sought to hide their true motives behind an economic façade. When the first indications of the global financial credit crunch began to be felt in the autumn of 2007, the Euro at first appeared to be immune. Its supporters insisted that it was a pillar of stability.

When Northern Rock came close to collapse and was nationalised in February 2008, the EU zealots were gleeful at the problems being suffered by the Dollar and the Pound Sterling. In the autumn of 2008 Lehman Brothers went bust, other banks collapsed into crisis and the London Stock Market plunged. Oh, how the Euro enthusiasts gloated.

What made it all so galling was that superficially the evidence at the time seemed to indicate that they might be correct. I and others knew that there were underlying problems in the Eurozone lurking beneath the surface, but in late 2008 they were not yet visible to the casual observer. Then in late November the President of the EU Commission, Jose Barroso, went a step too far in his gloating. In response, I fired off a blog entry from my office in Brussels in high dudgeon.

Name the guilty men!

The President of the European Commission Jose Manuel Barroso has said that Britain would be better placed to face the global credit crunch if we had joined the euro, and that serious people in the UK are defying public opinion and thinking in terms of British membership. He says he will "respect the confidentiality of private conversations", but that prominent British politicians have told him we should be better off in the euro.

This is not good enough. He cannot proceed by innuendo in this way. He needs to name the guilty men. Until he does, we are all under suspicion, so for the avoidance of doubt: I have not expressed that view to President Barroso, and my strongly-held opinion, both publicly and privately, is that we should avoid the euro like the plague.

The global credit crunch is a good example of the "asymmetric shock", which economists have warned could undermine the viability of the single currency. Britain has a much larger financial sector than any eurozone country, and will therefore react differently to global conditions. We absolutely need the currency flexibility to respond appropriately. Yes, the Pound has lost value compared with the dollar and the euro. If it had not, if we had been locked into the euro, our country and our exporters would be suffering from the effects of an over-valued currency.

Far from providing a reason for Britain to join the euro, the global crisis represents an existential threat to the survival of the single currency project. We have seen bond spreads between southern European countries, especially Greece, on the one hand, and Germany on the other, reach unprecedented and unsustainable levels. The question is not whether the euro can survive, but which eurozone member will be the first to leave. The euro is headed for a crisis, and we should thank heaven that we will not be there when the break-up comes.

The Pound does indeed face a serious threat, but that threat comes not from our position outside the euro, but from Gordon Brown's recession and Alistair Darling's profligate and unsustainable borrowing. This is a Labour crisis made in Britain.

Now blog entries are all very well. They make me feel better – especially those fired off like that – and they serve to make my position clear to anyone who cares to look. But there is nothing like telling a man to his face what you think of him. I got my chance on 13th January 2009 at the Plenary Session of the EU Parliament.

The EU Parliament loves to hold debates on subjects that are not up for discussion. I suppose it saves them having to debate anything of any real importance. Anyway, at this meeting the EU Parliament chose to hold a debate celebrating the ten years since the Euro was introduced as a shadow currency. Debate on the real review of assorted new laws was cut to make way for this debate.

The debate opened in predictable fashion with the usual suspects making grand speeches glorifying the Euro and explaining how clever the EU had been to invent the wretched thing. Well, I wasn't having that. When it was my turn I got up and said:

Mr. President

In the last two hundred years there have been at least half a dozen attempts to create monetary unions and fixed exchange rate systems. All have failed. All have damaged the participants. So it is with the euro. The imbalances long predicted by sceptics are starting to bite.

Italy's competitiveness is shot to pieces. Spain's experience is like the Bull in the Corrida: strong and proud at the start: *bleeding to death on the sand by the end. Greece's recent unrest clearly relates to high unemployment linked to an over-valued euro.*

Bond spreads between Greece and Germany have reached unprecedented levels – over 200 basis points. The markets are speculating on a euro-break-up.

We in Britain can thank Heaven that we kept our own currency, and are not part of the euro-zone's slow-motion train crash.

Rather unexpectedly the debate served to cause something of a spat in the European parliament. The problems then beginning to occur in Italy, Spain and Greece caused some caustic remarks to be made even by those in favour of the Euro. The Greeks did not appreciate this and called up a storm. They sent a memo round to all MEPs. As I blogged at the time:

The Greek MEPs claim that Greece has just successfully raised over € 2.5 billion in a new bond issue, at an average interest rate of only 2.51%. They cited this as evidence of the "credibility of Greece's performance as a trustworthy member of the

twitter

Now we have two eurozone countries living on borrowed money -- and borrowed time. Will Greece repay in three years? Will pigs fly?

Eurozone". But of course no government in Europe could place bonds at that rate in today's climate. In fact the new borrowing was not government bonds at all, but rather short term-paper and three-month notes.

I have fired back a new memo pointing out that the reliance on massive short-term financing is evidence not of Greece's "trustworthiness", but of the very severe difficulties that Greece faces in the bond market.

It is very worrying that these eleven Greek MEPs are pontificating about the eurozone, and about their country's financial position, when they seem to have little understanding at all of the basics of international finance. The eurozone is facing very serious challenges, and influential parliamentarians in Brussels and Strasbourg don't even start to understand the problem".

As the months passed the economic crisis gradually unfolded. Banks across Europe got into trouble and had to be bailed out by governments desperate to avoid a collapse. Recession bit, businesses failed and unemployment soared. Of particular concern to those supporting the Euro was the slow development of the sovereign debt crisis. Put simply the various member states within the Eurozone had been borrowing money on the international money markets in a most unwise fashion. Backed by the apparently stable and reliable Euro, the governments of some

twitter

Estonia joins the euro: they thought they were invited to a wedding, but it turned out to be a funeral.

BELOW: One of the ongoing absurdities of the EU Parliament is the monthly move from Brussels to Strasbourg. The regular move costs a fortune and wastes a huge amount of time. The French insist on it as they want to have EU Parliamentary meetings in France, and because they see Strasbourg as a symbol of Franco-German friendship (or enmity depending on how you look at it). Here I am campaigning against the charade in October 2010 with Lydia Smith, Oldrich Vlasak (Czech MEP) and an ECR staffer.

countries had borrowed far more than they could realistically pay back in a sensible time frame. International investors began to be wary of lending any more to these governments. Yet they needed to continue to borrow, some times simply to cover existing loans that were falling due.

The first country to be hit was Greece. On 27 April the Greek government debt rating was downgraded dramatically, to reach the junk status so greatly feared by governments the world over. There was a real fear that the Greek government might default on its debts. On 3 May the European Central Bank

took the step of effectively underwriting Greek bonds. That was not enough and the Eurozone countries agreed a €110 billion rescue package for Greece. They demanded in return a package of spending cuts and tax rises by the Greek government. Riots broke out across Greece and three people were killed.

The focus then shifted to Portugal, Spain and Italy which had similar debt problems to Greece. Those countries introduce austerity measures and received tacit support from the European Central Bank. Disaster was averted. For now. As the Americans say "They have just kicked the can down the road".

On Sunday 6th June the Sunday Telegraph ran the headline "The Euro will be dead in five years" in its business section. The story contained a survey of leading economists which backed up the headline. I am afraid that I could not resist the temptation and blogged at once.

Four of the nastiest words in the English language are surely "I told you so". They exude smug self-satisfaction. Yet in this case, and after years of heated debate, they are perhaps justified.

We sceptics have been arguing the case against monetary union for a dozen years. We said it was a political ploy, driven by hubris and ideology, and fraught with economic risk. The EU was not an optimal currency area. The Euro would be vulnerable to asymmetric shocks.

Yet we were dismissed by the Europhiles (and by some in the Conservative Party) as reactionary, fuddy-duddy, hopelessly out of touch, missing the zeitgeist of the times, isolationists who failed to understand economics or globalisation. In retrospect I think we understood economics and globalisation rather better than the Big Brains in the Berlaymont Building.

I recall my first radio debate as a euro-candidate, in 1999 at BBC Radio Leicester, up against Northamptonshire Labour MEP Angela Billingham (now ennobled – I always thought she looked rather like a ship in full sail, with her assistants bobbing along behind her). She argued that the euro was inevitable. It was progressive. It was the future. She understood, she said (she was extraordinarily patronising) the fearfulness of elderly people faced with change, but fortunately (she continued), young people embraced the euro as they back-packed to the delights of Prague and Krakow. I was able to cut her off at the knees with some very up-to-date opinion research showing that young people were, if anything, more sceptical of monetary union than their parents. This is surely an example of "The Wisdom of Crowds" – the instinctive common sense of ordinary people was right, where the careful and sophisticated analysis of the technocrats was wrong.

It has not been an easy decade for sceptics. For much of the Noughties, the euro seemed to be doing quite well.

"Where are the disasters, the asymmetric shocks you promised us?" demanded the Europhiles. As we see, they're here, and they're now. There are parallels here with the Soviet Union. For the euro in the Noughties, or the USSR in the Seventies, we knew intellectually that they were unsustainable and could not last, yet in our hearts we doubted. Both the euro and the USSR managed to exude such an aura of permanence and inevitability. Yet the USSR has gone, and the euro is going even as we speak. Both sought to impose centralised technocratic solutions on the hearts and minds of disparate nations. Both failed.

Cameron and Hague are right to point out that the potential collapse of the euro, and the political upheaval that will follow, in our largest trading partner, are not going to be good for Britain either. There are tough times ahead, which will challenge the coalition and especially George Osborne. Yet our ace-in-the-hole is an independent currency. There may be trouble ahead (as the song says), but nothing like the trouble we'd see if we were in the single currency. For that, if for nothing else, we have Gordon Brown to thank. And we sceptics must not let the chaos ahead sully our satisfaction at such a clear vindication of our long-held position. We were right, and we stuck to our guns even when it seemed unfashionable.

Over the summer of 2010 the rescue package was put into effect. The Euro rose on the exchange markets and the banking system stabilised. It proved to be an illusion. As the true scale of the debt problems in Spain, Italy and Portugal became clear, the Euro slumped again. On 16th November I blogged again.

Euro: the End-Game?

The situation with regard to the euro is becoming ever more surreal. The Portuguese Finance Minister Fernando Teixeira has said that "Contagion is spreading" and that "The whole eurozone is at risk". No less an authority than German Chancellor Angela Merkel (remember Germany's almost religious zeal for European union?) has said: "If the euro fails, then Europe will fail", and goes on to regret the possible demise of European values (though why these should depend on the currency, or on the EU, is not clear).

Yet I am told that the European President Rumpy Pumpy, that distinguished Belgian, while admitting that we face a crisis, nevertheless reassures all those around him that the EU has a plan, and that all will be well. And against this background, Estonia, a small Baltic state where I did a certain amount of work around the time of their EU accession referendum, is being dragged screaming into the eurozone against its will. As usual, the leadership of the country wants to parade its euro-credentials, while two thirds of the voters wisely oppose euro membership.

Strasbourg parliament: The Commission is about to address us on economic governance, while the eurozone implodes. Ironic or what?

It is bizarre that while we watch the currency's slow-motion train crash, there are actually countries proposing to join. The improbable image of rats boarding a sinking ship comes to mind, though the rats in this case are the politicians, not the populace (great folk, the Estonians).

Meantime wise voices like that of Jeremy Warner, the Telegraph's economic commentator, rightly warns against schadenfreude (while avoiding the German word). While celebrating the fact that we never joined the euro, he points out that the EU is our largest trading partner, and that the bloc's probable melt-down will do the British economy, and our recovery hopes, and our deficit reduction plan, no good at all. Of course he's right.

And yet, and yet... The demise of the euro, and therefore of the EU as we know it, will of course be a huge vindication of all I have believed and worked for over the last dozen years. And there might be a longer-term silver lining. If the collapse of the EU finally forces Britain, after forty years of introspective involvement in Europe, to focus our attention on the wider world — on China, India, the USA, the Commonwealth — then we may at last

have a chance to re-establish our status as a great trading nation, and share in some part of the future growth of the non-European world.

The future beckons. Europe is the past. There's a whole new world out there.

The next day I was at it again.

The euro crisis — which way for Greece?

For a long time I've pondered the position of Greece in the eurozone. They face disaster if they remain members. But then they face disaster if they leave. So which is the lesser evil?

I think I've resolved the matter in my mind, though I don't claim the same expertise in these matters as Jeremy Warner or Ambrose Evans-Pritchard.

It now seems certain that Greek bond-holders and creditors will be obliged to take a haircut, whether or not Greece stays in the euro-zone, though it is now clear that other euro-zone states fear for their own banks, which are heavily exposed to Greek debt. But from Greece's point of view, when they come to terms with the "haircut either way" scenario, the solution is pretty clear.

They can either apply the haircut (OK, let's be honest and call it "default"), but be stuck with an impossibly uncompetitive currency which will condemn them to grinding poverty *for the indefinite future. Or they can use their "Get Out Of Jail" card, and leave the euro.*

Either way, their reputation and their credit rating is shot. But in the second case, they have a reasonable prospect of an economic recovery within a few years.

So, Athens, time to cut the Gordian knot. And maybe the same advice applies to Lisbon and Dublin, while we're thinking about it.

The mention of Dublin was due to the sudden and unexpected crisis in Eire. The Irish boom – fuelled by unrealistically low interest rates due to membership of the Euro – had peaked in 2007. Unemployment had been growing ever since. The Irish government saw the problems and in 2008 had introduced a range of spending reductions, though these had done little to cut government debt. On the whole, all seemed to be calm on the surface. There were underlying problems, I think everyone knew that, but no immediate crisis was apparent.

Then the EU seemed to take fright. Rather inflammatory remarks were made by EU figures that caused confidence in the ability of the Irish government to meet its debts to wane. Having caused the crisis, the EU stepped forward to help. That help came with strings attached. Effectively Eire was losing its financial independence to Brussels. That was bad enough, but when David Cameron announced that Britain was joining in, I felt moved to blog again. It was 23rd November 2010.

Why the British loan to Ireland is wrong, wrong, wrong

• *We're told we have to support a good trading partner. That's like a business making a loan to an old customer who's gone bust, so that the customer can keep on buying. Not a good way to run a business. Or it's like trying to pull yourself up by your own boot-laces.*

• *You don't help an over-indebted country by forcing more debt on it. That's like forcing cocaine on to an addict.*

• *The £7 billion we propose to lend to Dublin is equivalent to all the cuts we're making in welfare.*

• *We don't have £7 billion. We're going to have to borrow it, adding to our own debt, to re-lend it to Dublin below market rates*

• *We may never see it back.*

• *It's around £300 for every household in Britain.*

• *This is not really about bailing out Ireland. It's about bailing out the euro. And the whole reason why we didn't want to join the euro in the first place was to avoid exactly this problem.*

• *We don't want to be part of a European debt union.*

Angela Merkel: "If the euro fails, then Europe will fail". Perhaps we can replace the EU with freedom, independence and democracy?

The only real solution for Ireland (and Greece) is to leave the euro. Now if Ireland were asking for help with a transition to a real, long-term solution, perhaps we should extend a helping hand.

But it was all a done deal. On 28th November Eire agreed to take the money from Brussels to solve a crisis sparked by Brussels and became the financial lap dog of Brussels. On 19th December I blogged

A lament for Irish Independence

Last week I attended an event in Strasbourg organised by my good colleague Nirj Deva MEP (South East Region). Nirj is a good Catholic gentleman, and he had invited the Irish Ambassador to the Holy See to come and address us. The meeting was well attended, especially by Irish MEPs.

I listened carefully to what the Ambassador had to say (I may have appeared to be doing the Telegraph crossword at the same time, but I find this an aid to concentration), and I was especially struck by his passing reference to the legal guarantees which were attached to the Treaty of Lisbon ahead of the second Irish referendum, which he said "ensured Ireland's independence". He said this, I noted, with a straight face and without any obvious hint of irony. Indeed he said it with a casual fluency which suggested that he had used the phrase often before, that he took it for granted, that he had never

thought to question it.

Where has he been for the last few months? In a monastery on Mount Athos? On a Trappist retreat? In Shangri-La? Wherever he's been, the rest of the world has looked on aghast as Ireland has been stripped of its fiscal and monetary independence, and has been forced into the humiliation of accepting, like it or not (and it was clear that Irish ministers didn't like it at all), a refinancing package cobbled together in Brussels, and designed not only to restore confidence in the Irish economy, but to create a firewall against contagion throughout the euro-zone.

Adding insult to injury, the initiative appears to have failed in its primary objective. Despite the refinancing, Moody's have just down-graded Irish sovereign debt, and the interest rate that the Irish government has to pay on its borrowings has reached eye-watering levels. Ireland has major debt-rollover issues in 2011, and it is by no means clear that it will be able to finance them.

Legal guarantees to protect Irish independence? When Ireland has, in fiscal terms, just been declared a protectorate of Brussels? I don't think so.

But the Ambassador might argue that he particularly had in mind those guarantees which apply not to fiscal policy, but to Ireland's distinctively Catholic stand on moral and ethical issues, like its position on abortion, where its restrictive laws force pregnant Irish women seeking a termination to go abroad. But sadly the news here is no better. We heard only yesterday that the European Court of Human Rights has ruled that Ireland's abortion laws breach the human rights of its citizens, and Ireland will be forced to change the law.

Now a purist might argue that the ECHR is not an institution of the EU, but of the Council of Europe, and thus that "clarifications" of the Lisbon Treaty could not have been expected to apply. But accepting the European Convention of Human Rights is a condition of EU membership, and the EU and the ECHR are now so intertwined that the distinction is (may I say?) Jesuitical.

So Ireland can no longer control its fiscal policy, nor manage its sovereign debt, nor even legislate for Catholic moral and ethical values. How much were those guarantees attached to Lisbon worth? Not a lot.

Some on this side of the Irish Sea may take a jaundiced view of Ireland's long struggle for independence from England, but it is a history which is woven into the fabric and the identity of Ireland, and in which (or at least in parts of which) the Irish people can take great and justifiable pride. Yet those who fought and died in that struggle must surely be turning in their graves as they see, after less than a century, the hegemony of London replaced by the

hegemony of Brussels. Farewell Irish independence. Today, Ireland is merely a remote off-shore province of Europe.

There are lessons here for the UK. David Cameron has just achieved in Brussels a political declaration, along with France and Germany, that the EU's "natural disasters" clause will never be invoked to require the UK to join in future euro-zone bailouts. This is a worthwhile achievement, and I would not denigrate it for a moment. But a political declaration carries less force than a legal guarantee, and we see how quickly Ireland's legal guarantees unravelled. I doubt that this reassurance carries any more weight than, for example, John Major's Maastricht opt-out on the Working Time Directive – and we saw how easily the Commission by-passed that one.

On 12th January 2011 we had a fascinating debate in our ECR Group meeting about a proposal currently going through the parliament. It covered a range of issues relating to economic management in the EU, and my good colleague Kay Swinburne MEP – who has forgotten more about the financial services industry than I ever knew – said that much of it is unexceptionable. But it included a proposal to create common eurozone debt instruments. Strictly speaking these would not be not "Eurobonds", since this phrase already meant something else. But we needed an easy handle for the new instruments, so Eurobonds they became. After the debate I blogged as follows:

The creation of these Eurobonds is intended to assuage the euro-zone crisis, by spreading the risk of dodgy peripheral countries of Portugal, Italy, Greece and Spain (the "PIGS") over the whole zone.

There is a straightforward (and simplistic) case for British MEPs to support the measure, and it goes like this: While we don't want to adopt the euro, we wish our EU partners well with the project, and we recognise that the UK economy would suffer from any dramatic collapse in the currency of our major trading partner. Therefore in a spirit of fraternal solidarity we should vote YES, to support our partners in their bold initiative to save the euro. OK, you've spotted the fallacy, but let's spell it out.

Spreading the contagion: These Euro-bonds will result in an averaging of risk, and interest rates, over the whole zone. So Portugal will be able to borrow more easily and cheaply. But the core countries will pay more for their debt, and be regarded by the markets as less secure than they were.

German public opinion: German voters are deeply opposed to taking more pain to bail out the profligate periphery. The German Constitutional Court is likely to rule on the legality of cross-border debt — I'm attending an Open Europe seminar in Brussels on this very subject later this morning.

Creating moral hazard: The PIGS have only been goaded into serious fiscal retrenchment because they're standing on the edge of a cliff. Make it easier for

twitter

Rumpy Pumpy (President of the EU): "We can't maintain a currency union without a political union". OK, Rumpy -- let's have neither.

them to borrow, and Greece will be back in its bad old ways. We'll simply be putting off the evil day when they face up to reality.

Building EU hegemony: This is another major step in building a financial infrastructure for a European State. It will be accompanied by all sorts of regulatory and other measures designed to achieve fiscal coordination, and it sits alongside plans for EU taxes and so on. We are fooling ourselves if we imagine that Britain would be unaffected by these measures, even if we're not in the eurozone. It will be a further ramping-up of the constant pressure to get deeper into the federal project.

There is an argument that says we should oppose the measure in a spirit of fraternal solidarity, because it is bad for the euro-zone; it damages our partners; it puts off vital and painful decisions; and it defers the necessity (in my view) to start on an orderly debt restructuring for the PIGS. We should be cruel to be kind.

I was delighted to find that the group overwhelmingly took the view that we should vote against. Special credit is due to our Polish and Czech colleagues.

Those countries could well "benefit" at some point from the lower interest rates within an EU debt union, yet they were quite clear on the principle, and firmly opposed to this new federalising measure.

And there, for now, the matter rests. The Euro has weathered the storm. But the underlying problems remain unsolved. The Euro is no more viable now than it was in 2008.

The price that has been paid by Eurozone countries for the survival of their currency has been the spreading of contagious debt and a massive transfer of power from the governments of member states to the central EU government in Brussels. But of course that is what the Brussels establishment has wanted all along: a centralised superstate with Brussels firmly in charge.

It looks as if they are getting their way.

BELOW: In March 2010 the Open Europe organisation held a fascinating debate in Brussels on the future of the EU. I was delighted to bump into Jonathan Isaby of the excellent ConHome website.

Comments on the Coalition

Those of you who have read this book thus far will have spotted in the previous two chapters that I am a Conservative MEP with an at times fraught relationship with the Conservative Party leadership – though not with its members. It is time to turn now to that subject.

I should first start by saying that I have voted Conservative all my life. It was my concern at the direction that the EU was going that prompted me to put my name forward for selection as an MEP. I have never made any secret of that fact, nor of my initial despair at the number of closet Europhiles that I found among the Conservative MEPs when I first arrived in Brussels in 1999.

I was deeply flattered to be selected at the No.1 position by the Conservative Party members in the East Midlands Region in that first election. Bill Newton-Dunn (from 1979 to 1994 MEP for Lincolnshire) was selected at No.2 and Chris Heaton-Harris, like me another new boy at No.3. Bill was one of those who loved the EU and all its works. Rather shockingly he betrayed the Conservative Party within a year of being elected and fled to the Liberal Democrats, whose Europhiliac policies were more in tune with his own. Ever since then I have thought of him as Bill Turncoat Dunn, and he still sits as a LibDem MEP. That left myself and Chris as Conservative MEPs for the East Midlands. We were re-elected in 2004, this time with Chris stepping up to be the No.2 candidate.

Ironically, within a year of that second election I myself ran into a problem. It was to become known through the East Midlands as the Reinstate Roger Row. I take no credit for the name, it was coined by others.

The trouble really began in July 2004 when Portuguese politician José Manuel Barroso was nominated as the new EU Commission president. In August 2004, he and his family enjoyed six days free hospitality on a luxury yacht owned by Greek shipping magnate and multi-billionaire Spiros Latsis. In September 2004, the Commission approved a € 10 million grant to the Lamda shipyard, in which Mr. Latsis has a substantial interest. Soon afterwards evidence began to emerge that Mr. Latsis's companies seemed to have other EU connections as well, not least through the then notorious Athens airport project.

On 24 May 2005, I blogged about the issue. Note that at this date Nigel Farage was not leader of UKIP, though he was leader of their MEPs.

President Barroso and the Motion of Censure

On Monday May 9th, in the opening plenary session of a Strasbourg week, UKIP MEP Nigel Farage called for a change in the week's agenda to allow a debate on this apparent conflict of interests. There was an electronic vote on Farage's proposal which was lost by a huge margin, all the main political groups opposing it.

We Conservatives were instructed by the Whips' Office not to vote. Don't vote Yes. Don't vote No. Don't even abstain. Sit on your hands and do nothing. Nevertheless, I and Chris Heaton-Harris defied the whip and voted Yes. We both believed that our 2004 Manifesto commitment to oppose fraud and corruption in the EU institutions required us to vote Yes.

Farage, and his Independent Democrats (ID) group, then initiated a Motion of Censure. Such a motion requires 10% of MEPs (74 members) to sign, in order to be formally tabled and debated. MEPs from many countries and groups signed. But the major political groups in the parliament, including the EPP-ED group (to which British Conservatives are affiliated -- some reluctantly) started ferocious campaigns of pressure and intimidation to get members to withdraw their names. They were keen to avoid embarrassment to the EU project, especially ahead of the French Constitutional referendum on May 29th. So we had a bucket with holes in it -- new MEPs signing the censure motion, while others fell off the bottom.

Nevertheless, the Motion achieved sufficient signatures and was tabled. It seems likely that it will be debated in the Brussels mini-plenary session during week commencing May 23rd -- ahead of the French referendum. Hans-Gert Pöttering, the President of the EPP-ED group, declared in the "Conference of Presidents" that none of his members

had signed -- or that if they had, they would withdraw their names. But at least six EPP-ED members had signed -- all British Conservatives. They were Chris Heaton-Harris, Dan Hannan, Martin Callanan, David Sumberg, Theresa Villiers (although there is some ambiguity about Theresa's status as an MEP following her election as MP for Chipping Barnet) and myself.

So Pöttering put pressure on the Conservative leader Timothy Kirkhope MEP, and he in turn wrote to the signatories demanding that they withdraw their names, and threatening "very serious consequences" -- parliament-speak for withdrawal of the Whip -- in the event of non-compliance.

Timothy's reasons for calling for our dissociation from the motion are instructive.

There is no firm evidence against Barroso. *But we never said there was. In a very soft motion, we merely point out a prima facie conflict of interests, and call on Barroso to come to the parliament and explain himself. We made it explicit that if he gave a satisfactory explanation we would withdraw the motion.*

We should not support another group's initiative. *Why not? We should read the message, not shoot the messenger. It would have been better if it had been our initiative. But if all the delegation had signed it, as we should have, we should have been the largest* *group of signatories and it would effectively be "our" initiative.*

We should not be associated with UKIP or Sinn Fein. *But when we voted against the EU Constitution in Strasbourg recently, we voted with UKIP and Sinn Fein. Every time we vote, every time we sign a Written Declaration, we are inevitably joined with a motley group of other MEPs, with many of whom we may profoundly disagree on many issues. In fact there is a strong correlation between our voting record and UKIP's, because we both oppose further European integration. The logic of Kirkhope's position would lead us not to vote on, or sign, anything.*

We should not oppose Barroso, because Barroso is promoting a centre-right agenda. *(Kirkhope and others have said this verbally, but have not written it down). So to paraphrase, we should oppose corruption if it comes from socialists, but not if it comes from the centre-right (so called)? Not an honourable position.*

Signing risks bringing the Conservative Party into disrepute. *Wrong. NOT SIGNING risks bringing the Party into disrepute. It is a clear and direct breach of a manifesto commitment.*

Kirkhope's letter set a deadline of noon on Thursday May 19th for names to be withdrawn. But none was withdrawn by that deadline.

So the motion stood, and came before a plenary session of the parliament, and Barroso was required to come to the parliament and explain himself. Barroso had brought the whole of his Commission to support him. The press gallery, sensing scandal, was packed. The format chosen for the debate was that Barroso would speak, followed by the leaders of the political groups in turn, in order of size. But there would be no general debate, and no opportunity for MEPs (other than group leaders) to speak.

This is a common format in the parliament, but on this occasion it meant, of course, that no Conservative would speak at all. As members of the EPP group, Hans-Gert Poettering would speak for us, and his one concern was to protect the Commission President (also affiliated to the EPP) and to protect the European project – especially with the French referendum on the Constitution only days away.

I was deeply frustrated that I should not be able to speak, and I turned to the fount of all knowledge on the Rule-Book, who was (of all people) Labour MEP Richard Corbett. A committed Europhile, he was also an anorak on parliamentary rules and procedures (and, to be fair, quite a decent chap if you could get over his ideological views).

twitter

Cameron wants free schools and personal responsibility. Clegg/Cable want an intrusive top-down university admissions policy. Doesn't stack.

So I e-mailed him to ask if there was any way I could intervene in the debate. His cryptic reply was "Read Rule 121". I did.

Rule 121 (which so far as I know had never been invoked before, and of which I had never heard) allowed any member to seek to intervene during another member's speech, with a question. But both the speaker and the President of the parliament were entitled to refuse the request. Now the only group leader who would speak in favour of the motion and against Barroso would be Nigel Farage, as leader of the (then) ID group, so he was the only speaker who might be inclined to take my question. So I approached him and warned him that I would seek to intervene in his speech. I regarded this as simply a normal parliamentary courtesy. Kirkhope subsequently chose to regard it as colluding with the enemy.

Come the day, I stood and made my request. Farage was quite happy to give way, but to my surprise and disappointment, the acting President of the session, Spanish MEP Alejo Vidal-Quadras, refused to allow my intervention. I sat down disappointed. But then at the end of Farage's speech, Vidal-Quadras said "Now, Mr. Helmer, you may ask your question – I didn't want to deprive Mr. Farage of his speaking time". So I asked my question, which was a strongly-worded

twitter
Cameron dumps multiculturalism. And about time too

condemnation, primarily of Poettering for seeking to sweep the issue under the carpet, and for putting pressure on MEPs to withdraw their names from the motion, but also of Kirkhope for colluding with Poettering and pressuring the Conservative signatories.

As soon as I had finished, Poettering leapt to his feet, apoplectic. So far as I can remember, he said something along the lines of "That's enough! I've given this man plenty of leeway, but this is too much! He's fired! He is no longer a member of our EPP group!".

Poettering was immediately surrounded by his own officials, who appeared to be reminding him that under the EPP group rules he simply didn't have the authority to fire an EPP member in a fit of pique. He had to go through due process. Accordingly, an extraordinary group meeting was called for the next week, at which I was invited to speak in my defence. I daresay that the assembled group was expecting a grovelling apology and a plea for leniency, but that wasn't quite what they got:

Mr. President,

I should like to start by apologising, to Mr. Kirkhope. If I caused him offence I regret that.

Back in 1999, on my first day in this parliament, I decided that I was sitting in the wrong group, and I have campaigned unsuccessfully against British membership of the EPP ever since. The only reason that I did not resign years ago was a sense of Party loyalty and discipline. I may add that my respect for Party loyalty and discipline seem to have attracted very little credit or gratitude.

I therefore welcome this motion today. Six years on, it seems that you have come round to my own view, that I can no longer sit in the group.

There are two clear reasons for this. First, on many issues the group is to the left, not only of the British Conservatives, but of the British Labour government as well. Take the Working Time Directive. Mrs Oomen Ruiten is a lady of great personal charm, but as coordinator on employment she argued for a left-wing position and took a large part of the group with her. Her predecessor Bartho Pronk took a similarly socialist line.

Secondly, the issue of Europe. Many of my British colleagues, with typical British courtesy, try to avoid stressing Conservative policies that might give offence. So when I stress those policies, I may seem, here in Strasbourg, to be in a minority. No doubt today, as usual, my friend and colleague Chris Beazley will pop up like a comedy cliché to contradict me. Yet I am merely stating policies which you could read in our election manifesto a few weeks ago.

In the Motion of Censure debate, Hans-Gert, speaking on behalf of the whole group including British Conservatives, you said that no one, but

twitter

Ed Balls says that George Osborne is "doing everything that Thatcher did". To which the only reply is, "If only!"

no one, must seek to undermine our resolve as we build European integration. Yet again, you chose to ignore your commitment to respect our distinct position on constitutional matters.

The Conservative Party is opposed to further European integration. We have explicit manifesto commitments to oppose the euro and the Constitution. Yesterday in the House of Commons, our shadow Foreign Minister Liam Fox, a former doctor, speaking about the Constitution, said "I have not practiced medicine for some years, but I still know a corpse when I see one". Conservatives rejoiced at the outcome of the French and Dutch referendums. We are committed to start dismantling the European construction, returning key powers from Brussels to member-states.

I have had a bigger mail-bag on the Motion of Censure than I have ever had on any issue over six years. I have received literally hundreds of messages, from members of the House of Commons and the Lords, from Constituency Chairmen, Councillors, Party agents, members and activists, from up and down my region and indeed across the UK. Not one has opposed my stand.

Indeed they are uncannily similar. The same phrases keep recurring: "Stick to your guns", "Don't back down", "Thank you for supporting our principles", "You're saying what we're thinking". That's the Conservative Party I'm proud to represent.

Last week, the Daily Telegraph published a poll taken amongst Party members. They were asked what views on Europe they would like to see in our new leader, and were offered a scale from "Staunch euro-sceptic" through to "Staunch euro-phile". Over half of them, an absolute majority, opted for "Staunch euro-sceptic". And how many chose "Staunch euro-phile"? Ten percent? Five percent? Two percent? No. ZERO PERCENT! That's the Conservative Party I represent.

So I urge colleagues to support this motion, since it represents one point on which we can agree. But I urge you to support it for another reason as well. Two weeks ago Hans-Gert, rather prematurely, and in front of the parliament, the whole Commission and much of the world's press, announced the result of today's vote! If we fail to pass this motion now, we will cut the ground from under his feet. We will cause him great embarrassment. I have no wish to do that.

Finally, may I address a few words especially to my British colleagues? We are reaching a turning-point. The wind is changing. Last week, two founder members of the EU resoundingly rejected European integration. Last week, German industry minister Wolfgang Clement said "the euro is strangling our industry" – and he should know! Last week in Italy, the Northern League called for Italy to leave the euro-zone and re-adopt the Lira. A major international bank has said that Italy faces "horrible martyrdom" in the euro-zone.

Last week we saw bond spreads widening between Germany and Italy. This represents a crack in the euro itself. And the Dutch, God bless 'em, rather than putting their finger in the dyke, gave two fingers to the entire project!

Across Europe, political leaders, financial institutions and ordinary voters are starting to realise that the European project has failed. We Conservatives are winning the argument. This is no time for us to be sitting with a federalist group.

I was duly expelled from the EPP. And a good thing too. I never looked back. The suspension of the Conservative whip was another matter entirely. Nirj Deva, Conservative MEP for London, was quick to argue that the whip should be restored. His views were reported in the London Evening Standard less than a week after the vote in the EPP. Chris Heaton-Harris and other MEPs joined him, but the subject remained for some time restricted to those following events within the British delegation in Brussels.

At the time the Conservative Party as

twitter

Good luck today to our candidate in the Old & Sad by-election, Kashif Ali. He's gonna need it.

a whole was far more concerned with the leadership election that was expected to take place imminently following Michael Howard's poor showing in the 2005 General Election. Only one of the leadership contenders came from my East Midlands Region, and that was Ken Clarke. Ken is a great chap, but his pro-EU leanings are at odds with my own views, and some mischievous journalists tried to manufacture an issue involving my loss of the whip and Ken's leadership ambitions.

The leadership election ended, of course, with the victory of David Cameron on 6 December. I had backed Mr Cameron due to his pledge to remove the Conservative MEPs from the EPP and his pledge to hold a referendum on the EU Constitution. Most people expected the whip to be restored to me early in the new year, but this did not happen.

On 3rd March three young Conservative Party members launched a campaign under the heading of Reinstate Roger. The youngsters involved were Andrew Woodman, Chris Palmer and Richard Hyslop. Within weeks nearly 1,000 MPs, MEPs, councillors, party officials and party members had signed up to the website. Iain Dale's Diary took up the subject, as did many other political commentators and blogs. This work was entirely the

initiative of the three grassroots workers, although I was grateful for it.

Through all these months I remained a loyal Conservative. I campaigned in council elections across the East Midland, voted assiduously with the Conservative MEPs in the EU Parliament and supported David Cameron whenever a journalist asked my opinion (presumably hoping that since I did not have the whip I might say something unflattering). The idea of leaving the Conservative Party never once occurred to me. I had seen Bill Turncoat Dunn turn yellow by joining the LibDems. I had no intention of following his lead. I had been elected as a conservative and would remain a conservative, even if the Party leadership in Brussels did not want me. They would not get rid of me that easily.

The whip was eventually restored in September 2006, though I remained thankfully out of the EPP. I owe great thanks to many people for my reinstatement, not least the trio behind the Reinstate Roger website. In EU speak I was thus a non-inscrit MEP. This means that I was still a Conservative MEP, but not in any political group within the Parliament.

I found that there were great advantages in being Non-Inscrit, as compared to my previous status in the EPP.

I had greater access to parliamentary facilities – for example organising venues for meetings and conferences. Suddenly, I had more group staff – and they were working for me, not for the greater glory of the EU! I also had a great deal more funding. Each member of a recognised group receives around €75,000 a year in parliamentary funding. But normally the group takes a top slice – in the case of the EPP, around half. Then the national delegation takes a slice, which in the case of British Conservatives had to be quite a large slice, to enable us to hire delegation staff. These should have been provided by the EPP, but they were very reluctant to do so – an on-going source of friction. So we ended up with around €10,000 each in "Information Funding", to pay for advertising, leaflets and so on to support our regional work.

As a Non-Inscrit, however, I received €40,000 a year. That was less than the €75,000 for group members – but it all came direct to the member, with no one top-slicing it on the way.

But perhaps the biggest benefit was improved access to plenary speaking time. Suddenly, I was free to speak in practically any debate I wanted. Group members tend to be limited to their own Committee topics, and if the group doesn't like them, they may get no time at all. While Dan Hannan, for example, was on the Constitutional Affairs Committee, I believe the EPP gave him no speaking time at all – because they had a pretty good idea of what he would say.

This benefit came to the fore during the UK's EU Presidency in July,

December 2005. Tony Blair, as rotating President-in-Office for the six months, came no fewer than three times to the parliament. In each case he spoke, and a debate ensued, starting as always with speeches from group leaders.

Now of course the Non-Inscrit are not a group in the strict sense. They have no common ideological basis. Yet the parliament treats the Non-Inscrit as a group for administrative purposes, and this includes speaking time in the round of group leaders' speeches. The problem is that the Non-Inscrit, of course, have no leader. But that was my opportunity. On each of Tony Blair's visits, I argued that as a Brit, I had a special interest in speaking in the first round, and each time I managed to do so.

The first occasion was particularly amusing. No one in the Conservative delegation knew that I had speaking time. But in the plenary, there is an electronic screen with the names of the current speaker and the next three scheduled speakers. The Non-Inscrit are the smallest "group" and speak last, so about half way through the running order, my name popped up at the bottom of the screen. Timothy Kirkhope, as Conservative delegation leader, was sitting in the front row, and when my name appeared he jumped as though stung by a wasp. Immediately he was surrounded by his Chief Whip, his Deputy, and various minions, taking counsel together about how they might cope with this situation. If you'll forgive a second entomological simile, they looked like ants whose ant-hill has just had a good kick.

Hague: "Labour's handling of the Lisbon Treaty has caused deep anger". Yes. But so has Cameron's broken referendum promise.

ABOVE: During the 2010 Conservative Party Conference I took part in a debate in the Freedom Zone, run by the superb Freedom Association. The subject was the EU, so the logo of our new ECR Group was projected on to the screen behind me.

I managed to get in some good hits on Blair – at least he got quite cross, which I took as a good sign. But the icing on the cake was this: Blair only stayed to hear the first round of group leaders' speeches, of which mine was the last. And who was the next speaker? Why the leader of the second largest delegation in the largest group – none other than Kirkhope himself, speaking immediately after me. So Kirkhope enjoyed the dubious privilege of speaking to the back of a retreating Prime Minister as he left the chamber. Delightful.

In February 2008 I was to be joined outside the EPP by Dan Hannan, Conservative MEP for the Southeast Region of England. After the 2009 EU elections all Conservatives left the EPP and joined the new ECR Group.

In the run up to those 2009 elections I chaired a debate on the fringe of the 2008 Party Conference that asked the question "What Conservatives want in their euro-manifesto". The event was held courtesy of the Freedom Association. After the event I blogged as follows:

In the Freedom Zone at Party Conference, on Monday Sept 29th, I chaired a debate on the 2009 euro-manifesto, with a range of euro-candidates, plus major Party donor Stuart Wheeler. The Candidates were John ("Give Europe some Flack") Flack from Eastern England; Jean-Paul Floru from London (how cool would it be to send a Belgian euro-sceptic to Brussels to represent

London?); Therese Coffey from the South East; Zehra Zaidi from the South West, and our own Rupert Matthews from the East Midlands.

After a short introduction, we invited comments from the floor, and debated them. At the end, I checked that my understanding of the issues reflected the mood of the meeting, and promised that I would forward the findings to William Hague and Mark Francois. I am delighted to say that the meeting (just short of a hundred Conservatives) supported the consensus positions almost unanimously — and I learned afterwards that the only two No votes were from dissenters who wanted an even tougher line on EU issues.

To summarise briefly the views of the meeting:

EU Constitution/Lisbon Treaty: The meeting overwhelmingly supported the Party's position that if we form a government before Lisbon is fully ratified, we should hold a referendum on it, and accept the result. If it is fully ratified by all 27 member-states, we should undertake a radical re-negotiation of our EU membership, aiming for a new relationship based solely on free trade and voluntary intergovernmental cooperation. These steps should be immediate. Under no circumstances should they be labelled "2nd Term Issues".

Common Foreign and Security Policy: The meeting agreed that the CFSP is incompatible with national independence. While we support ad hoc cooperation and alliances, British foreign policy should be determined in Britain, by Britain, for Britain.

Trade Policy/WTO: The UK's trade policy is determined by Brussels, and is biased against the Anglo-sphere. Protectionist decisions are frequently made to protect (for example) Italian shoe-makers or Portuguese lingerie manufacturers, which are not in Britain's interests. Trade policy should be repatriated, with more emphasis on the Anglosphere.

Costs of EU membership: It was noted that credible estimates of the total cost of Britain's EU membership are put at £60 billion a year. This may have been affordable in good economic times. It is unsustainable in the face of a global financial crisis. The Party should commit to a government White Paper on the costs and benefits of EU membership.

Common Fisheries Policy: It was recalled that under Michael Howard's leadership, and based on a very thorough analysis by Owen Paterson MP, the Party was committed to reasserting control over Britain's fisheries and territorial waters, and withdrawing from the appalling CFP. The meeting called for that policy to be explicitly reinstated.

twitter

"Coalition Candidates" at the next
General Election? They won't get my
support -- or my vote.

Freedom of Information Act:
*It was proposed that a measure similar
to the UK Freedom of Information Act
should be brought forward in the EU, to
end the culture of secrecy surrounding
EU policy and decision-making.*

Strasbourg: *The Party should
have an explicit policy of a single seat
in Brussels for the European
parliament, eliminating the ludicrously
expensive monthly commuting to
Strasbourg.*

*No doubt others will have additional
ideas, but these, surely, would be a good
start, and would have the backing of
Conservatives and of a broad swathe of
public opinion.*

At the time none of this was contrary
to Conservative Party policy on the EU,
though much of it was simply not
mentioned by the Party in explicit policy
terms. At any rate, it served to show how
the grass roots of the Party viewed the
EU.

One subject which had not really
come up much at the meeting was the
ongoing issue of the Conservative MEPs
being members of the EPP. The party
and David Cameron had a long standing
commitment to take us out of the EPP,
but this had not yet been achieved. Left
wing commentators – on the BBC and

in the Guardian – were having much glee
speculating that we could find no other
MEPs wanting to join a group with us.
And there were some pro-EU MEPs and
others in the party who made little secret
of the fact that they thought we should
remain in the EPP. Frankly it was all
getting a bit embarrassing.

Then in March 2009 David Cameron
came good on his promise. I blogged on
12th March about the dramatic new
move.

The EPP: Cameron delivers

*Yesterday, at a meeting of the UK
Conservative delegation in Straz,
William Hague and Mark Francois,
fresh from a meeting with EPP Group
President Joseph Daul, announced that
they had given formal notice to the
EPP that Conservative MEPs would
leave the EPP group at the end of this
parliamentary term, in three months'
time. This should not be news at all,
since David Cameron and William
have repeatedly confirmed the intention,
but none-the-less it was good to hear
that the formal process was in place.*

*Labour have a Leader who (inter
alia) promised an end to boom'n'bust,
and a referendum on the European
Constitution. He did not deliver. We
have a leader who promised to take us
out of the EPP, and despite delays, he is
now delivering. I voted for Cameron in
our Conservative leadership election
mainly because of his commitment on
the EPP, and I am delighted to see it
fulfilled.*

ABOVE: I spent the general election campaign of 2010 out pounding the pavements with our excellent team of candidates. This is my visit to Broxtowe, where I bumped into our East Midlands Regional Chairman Linda Kirk (centre). Our candidate Anna Soubry went on to win.

I had just tumbled off an overnight flight from New York via London, and hadn't even had time to change, so I attended the meeting dishevelled, tie-less and unshaven, but I relished the occasion none-the-less.

This news on the EPP is surely of no interest -- meaningless indeed -- to the great majority of voters, who know nothing of the EPP and care even less. Yet to political anoraks and activists, and to Brussels insiders, it is momentous news. It is a touchstone issue. As I have

been asked a hundred times: how can you pretend to be a eurosceptic Party when you sit with the Group that calls itself "the motor of European integration"? This is a story that has run for at least ten years -- the whole of my parliamentary career. When I was first elected in 1999, the Party announced a new, arm's length relationship with the EPP ("merely sharing an administrative umbrella"), and I thought in my naïveté that we had won the battle.

So you can imagine my rage and disappointment at our first delegation meeting in July 1999 when our then Leader Edward McMillan Scott announced (as near as I can remember): "Well that's all sorted out then -- back to business as usual". That precipitated a row that ran on and off for years until Cameron lanced the boil.

Of course people are now asking "So who's in your new group, then?" The answer is that these are sensitive political issues for all the parties involved, and our new partners will want to time their own announcements to suit their own domestic political agendas. It would be quite improper for us to jump the gun. So watch this space. We will be forming a new, centre-right, non-federalist Party in the new parliament, and I look forward very much to joining it.

My time after this was largely taken up with campaigning for the Conservative Party in the East Midlands. Due to the arcane candidate selection rules imposed by the national party, I was selected as No.1 Candidate yet again but this time without the ordinary party members getting a choice. As the sole incumbent MEP re-standing (Chris Heaton-Harris was standing down to pursue his ambitions to become a national MP) I automatically topped the list. The rest of the team of candidates was, in order, Emma McClarkin, Rupert Matthews, Fiona Bulmer and George Lee. I was delighted with the result.

Once again the Conservatives won two MEPs in the East Midlands, so Emma and I were elected. Labour got one MEP, UKIP one and Bill Newton Dunn again just scraped in as the sole LibDem MEP. With the EU elections out of the way, all eyes turned to the coming General Election. Emma and I

got down to work in Brussels, and also campaigned alongside our Conservative MP candidates whenever we got the chance.

In April 2010, I turned my attention to the EU policies of the LibDems. I had a special interest as their new leader, Nick Clegg, had been LibDem MEP for the East Midlands from 1999 to 2004 and I knew him and his views reasonably well. At the time I wrote

Nick Clegg on the EU: Wrong, and arguably dishonest

As Nick Clegg's star appears to rise, it is entirely right that other parties should draw attention to the damaging nature of Lib-Dem policies. We in the Conservative Party have pointed out that the Lib-Dems supported the defunct EU Constitution; supported the Lisbon Treaty (which amounts to the EU Constitution Mark 2); support (and indeed claim credit for) the EU Arrest Warrant, which is denying some UK citizens the most basic legal rights; and even favour scrapping the Pound and having Britain join the failing euro project. In fact the Lib-Dems have a knee-jerk response to any EU proposal: Vote Yes.

And Nick Clegg's answer to these accusations? Shocking, even by the

BBC Radio 4 Today Programme comment: "The Lib-Dems have five seats in Cabinet, and they get Ken Clarke for free".

mendacious standards of the Lib-Dems. He asks (and I quote from today's papers) "Do we really think we can pull up the drawbridge, and (that) ranting and raving from the sidelines is really going to help us be stronger and safer?"

Who are these people who want to "pull up the drawbridge and rant and rave from the sidelines"? There may be a few in some fringe parties, but none that I have met in the Conservative

BELOW: On the night of the General Election itself I went to Daventry to support my former comrade in arms in Europe, Chris Heaton-Harris in his bid to become MP for Daventry. I was delighted to see that Chris has won, and must say that he is shaping up to be an excellent MP.

Party. We are a Party of free trade, and not given to pulling up drawbridges. We would like to see global free trade, but failing that, free trade across Europe is a good start (although many of us regret that the EU is, of course, not a free trade area but a customs union). We are an internationalist Party (although unlike the Lib-Dems, we recognise that there is a world beyond Brussels). So we are strongly in favour of international cooperation, both with EU countries and with non-EU countries, in dealing with all the issues that cross borders, like crime, terrorism, trade, pollution and so on.

So where are our differences with Clegg? Simply that while we want

trade and cooperation, we also want to participate as a free, independent and democratic nation, not as an off-shore province in a quasi-country called Europe, which is neither democratic nor accountable. The EU has a malign momentum of its own, and (as we have seen in referendum after referendum) it treats the will of the people with utter contempt. Even Clegg admits, with masterful understatement, that the EU "is not a model of democratic efficiency".

The implicit falsehood in the Lib-Dem position is the assumption, absurd when you spell it out, that we can only achieve trade and cooperation if we sacrifice independence and democracy.

And Clegg knows this. During the time when we both sat in the European parliament representing the East Midlands (1999/2004), I several times debated against him. I vividly recall him remarking to me (he now conveniently insists that he has no recollection of the statement, but I remember it very clearly) "When I first heard your views on Europe, Roger, I thought you were mad. But now that I've heard you argue your case, I can see that you have an intellectually defensible position, even though I disagree with it". So he knows that no one in the Conservative Party wants to "Pull up the drawbridge and rant and rave". And his deliberate use of this mendacious caricature is downright dishonest.

twitter

"Equality": Positive discrimination in the workplace? This Coalition is no better than Labour on these issues. I'm ashamed of it.

The General Election campaign rushed on. Looking back I think I must have been too busy pounding pavements and hammering on doors to bother blogging, issuing press releases or even updating the website. Certainly I did not write much, and I do recall getting blisters. The election was held on Thursday 6th May 2010 and I spent most of the day supporting my former MEP colleague Chris Heaton Harris in his bid to win Daventry. I spent the night at the Daventry count, which seemed to drag on forever, but Chris won by a huge margin.

As we all know, no single party got an overall majority nationally. There were negotiations between Gordon Brown, still Prime Minister until another emerged, and Nick Clegg as they tried to patch up a Labour-LibDem coalition. Then we heard that David Cameron was also talking to Nick Clegg. I blogged on the subject as the talks continued.

General Election 2010: The dust settles

We are all, of course, horribly disappointed that we failed to get the majority Conservative government for which we had worked and campaigned for so long. Yet we should not belittle the scale of our achievement: we all knew we had an electoral mountain to climb, and that the system was stacked against us, yet we gained nearly 100 seats. I could scarcely believe the early projections based on exit polls, and as some of the early results came in those projections looked even more suspect. Yet by breakfast time on Friday, we saw that they had been bang on the money.

Nevertheless, we are where we are, in a hung parliament, and it seems to me that we have two imperatives. First, for our country we have to deliver stable governance and fiscal consolidation – and we have to do that quickly. So Cameron is right to talk to Clegg. Like many Conservatives, I personally hate the idea of having to do a deal with the Lib-Dems. I hate their cynicism, their opportunism, their mendacity. I hate the way they will tell diametrically opposite stories in adjacent constituencies – or even on adjacent doorsteps. They will say anything to get elected – in the debates, Clegg even denied policies which were there in black and white in his manifesto. Yet with them, we should have an overall majority in the Commons. And anyway, I should also hate the pork-barrel politics of paying vast and unaffordable sums to Northern Ireland as the price for cooperation from the Unionists, even though in so many ways they would be much more agreeable bedfellows.

I am pleased that Cameron has drawn clear red lines on Europe, immigration and defence. He was right to do so. I am very comfortable with

twitter

Martin Callanan elected new Leader of the Tory MEP delegation. Excellent result. Fox & McClarkin elected to the Bureau.

moves to reduce taxes for the low-paid – we should have been doing that anyway. I am much less happy about the green agenda, but I suppose we have to make concessions somewhere, and the green agenda may well fall apart as the global warming "consensus" continues to disintegrate. Certainly it is way down the public's priority list. On electoral reform, there is much we can and should do without giving way on PR.

Our second imperative, for our Party, is to regroup for the next General Election, which if previous precedents are followed will occur well before 2015, and maybe this year. And for this reason we must avoid recrimination. Given our disappointment at the result, it would be all too easy to start looking for scapegoats. Easy, but wrong. We must learn the lessons of this campaign, but we must not tear ourselves apart. We certainly made some mistakes.

As I understand the constitutional position, the incumbent Prime Minister has the first opportunity to see if he can form a government. (Do we have an incumbent Prime Minister, you may well ask? Hasn't Gordon Brown resigned? He seems to have half-resigned). The key test comes later this month, when some kind of Queen's

Speech or programme for government has to be presented to the Commons. If that succeeds, the government can continue indefinitely (until 2015), or until it falls on a vote of confidence. If it fell, the Queen would call on whomever she considered capable of forming an administration — clearly, in this case, David Cameron. He could then either seek coalition partners, or seek to operate a minority government.

I'm beginning to suspect that we might in fact get a fragile Lib-Lab coalition.

The consequence would be great public anger and resentment against both parties in this "coalition of losers". The public would see a Lib-Lab pact as, first, a failed Labour administration clinging to power by its fingernails with a shabby deal; and second, a Lib-Dem party propping up a Labour administration which the voters had roundly rejected. So neither would look good — and both would attract opprobrium for the budgetary measures they would be forced to take.

We'd probably see a second General Election in October, in which I could well imagine a majority Conservative government being formed. So I would not see an immediate Lib-Lab pact as a disaster by any means.

Time to put my hands up. I was wrong about a Labour-LibDem coalition. Even as I wrote the talks behind closed doors were going wrong.

A Conservative-LibDem coalition was becoming increasingly likely. I blogged again 24 hours later.

The tables are turned: It's the Con-Lib coalition

As Harold Wilson never said, twenty-four hours is a long time in politics. Yesterday morning, I was writing ruefully about the Lib-Lab "coalition of losers" that looked increasingly likely. Today, David Cameron is in Downing Street. Down the road, there are all sorts of questions about the durability of the coalition, and the public allocation of blame for the inevitable cuts, hardship and austerity. Labour's next campaign slogan could be "Remember we opposed the Tory cuts".

But for now (and for the first time in my twelve-year political career), we have a Conservative Prime Minister in Number Ten.

As Maggie Thatcher certainly did say, "Rejoice, rejoice, rejoice". Our hopes and aspirations go with you, Dave. Keep the faith.

By July I was starting to get a bit fed up with the way the coalition was shaping up. I had been bitterly

twitter🐦

Memo to George Osborne: You could save £20+ bn p.a. by abandoning our ludicrous "green energy" plans, and £100 bn by leaving the EU.

disappointed by the November 2009 decision by David Cameron to renege on his cast iron guarantee to hold a referendum on the Lisbon Treaty. I already had the feeling that David Cameron was drifting away from the core beliefs of the Conservative Party. Now I began to worry that the LibDems were having undue influence in the coalition. On 28th July I blogged as follows:

BELOW: In 2010 I was delighted to support the campaign group Stop Turbines at Ringstead (STAR) based in Northamptonshire. Wind turbines are a dreadful eyesore that cannot be justified in terms of electricity generation or environmental considerations.

Some minor carping from the sidelines

I yield to no one in my admiration for David Cameron. Just back from a successful trip to the States, he is now on a key mission to India, via Ankara. If he is not yet bestriding the world like a Colossus, he is at least well on the way. And he has made an excellent start to coalition government. Dealt a hand by the electorate that he may have preferred not to hold, he has made the best of it. He negotiated the coalition; he reassured the markets; he and his colleagues have made excellent moves on health, on education, on policing.

He has also, arguably, played a cool hand with the Lib-Dems. The inevitable opprobrium which will be engendered by the coming cuts will be easier to bear when shared, while the opinion polls show that so far we Conservatives are reaping far greater benefits than our partners. Conservatives always wondered what on earth was the point of voting Lib-Dem: now many Lib-Dem voters seem to be asking the same question.

Yet as some have pointed out, Cameron has two coalitions to worry about: that with the Lib-Dems, and that with his back benches. I would add a third: the coalition with his party members and activists. And here there are some issues that worry these folk.

Energy Security: The green Lib-Dem zealot Chris Huhne, who has been allowed to assume the role of Energy Secretary, is rushing to impose his anti-nuclear prejudices on the body politic. We have to recognise that an energy supply crisis in 2015 could cost the British economy as much as the banking crisis of 2008. On the associated issue of wind farms, a great number of good Conservatives are hopping mad at the way new on-shore turbines are approved.

Justice: I always used to say that I greatly admired Ken Clarke, apart from his Euro-mania. But like most Conservatives, I'm shocked by his approach to prison. It's great to look at non-custodial sentences, but Clarke doesn't seem to have realised that many of those sent to jail these days are there precisely because they declined to fulfil non-custodial sentences.

Taxation: George Osborne is proving one of the stars of the coalition. We face difficult times, so we can't cut taxes as we should. But we shouldn't be leaving pointless taxes in place merely for presentational reasons. Labour's 50% income tax is a retrograde step which will collect no extra revenue, but will slow growth and deter investment.

European Union: the perennial problem. We were elected on clear commitments to oppose future EU integration, to hold a referendum on future proposals, to provide a "triple lock", and to make a start on repatriating powers from Brussels. I understand the exigencies of coalition. But the indecent haste with which we are embracing EU integration is embarrassing. Three weeks back we MEPs in Brussels were whipped to vote for the European External Action Service (EEAS) – something we had always opposed. Then the next week on a similar vote in Westminster, Conservatives were again whipped to vote Yes. Next thing we hear is that Home Secretary Theresa May has approved the EU's Investigation Order,

twitter

For 11 years as an MEP in opposition I've waited for a new government to get a grip on the EU problem. How many more years?

which will allow foreign police forces access to DNA data, phone and bank data in the UK.

So my advice – my plea – to Cameron, and Hague, and Theresa May – is: Don't take your back-benchers for granted. Nor your Party members and activists out there. We didn't work our socks off for Huhne's wind farms, or for Labour taxes, or for Ken's prison policies, or for more EU integration. And we may think twice next time.

I was indeed carping from the sidelines. The coalition continued to drift leftwards, and I grew increasingly disturbed by the apparent relish with which Mr Cameron did this. Leader of the coalition he may be, but he is also leader of the Conservative Party. Come the Party Conference in October 2010 I felt moved to return to the subject in my blog. This time my heading was rather firmer, reading "Has the Coalition lost the plot on the EU?"

Earlier today I spoke to a packed Bruges Group fringe meeting in Birmingham, and I posed this question: Has the Coalition (and the Conservative Party) lost the plot on the EU? I'm afraid the answer is YES.

As a Conservative, I have for years received e-mails from constituents asking how I as a eurosceptic can remain in a party so obviously committed to the European project, and I have replied that the Party needs a bit

of Eurosceptic ballast, that I'm trying to keep it honest, that if all the sceptics leave then the pro-EU trend will get worse. And I've said that I hoped that Conservatives in government would prove the doubters wrong.

So where are we after five months of Conservative-led Coalition government? Last week Vince Cable told a Brussels audience that the EU institutions had been "pleasantly surprised" by the Coalition's engagement with, and commitment to the EU project. And for once Vince wasn't wrong. The truth is that we've been handing powers to Brussels under the Coalition arguably faster than Labour did before us. No wonder that the sound Shadow Europe Minister Mark François was replaced by the plausible and managerial David Lidington.

A couple of months back, we Conservative MEPs were whipped to vote in favour of the new EU diplomatic service, the EEAS, on "Instructions from London", despite having been elected on a 2009 Manifesto that explicitly committed us to opposing it. We had opposed the Lisbon Treaty that provides a legal basis for the EEAS, we had opposed the EEAS itself, and we were right to do so. The structures of a single country called the EU are being put in place around us, and we are now whipped to vote in favour on the specious basis that we'll have to work with it, so we'd better pretend to like it.

ABOVE: In July 2010 I took part in the Boston Tea Party, an event held in Boston (Lincs) to highlight the fact that we are already too highly taxed and that taxation rates should be reduced. From left to right: Robin Tilbrook (leader of the English Democrats Party), Derek Clark (MEP for UKIP), Rupert Matthews (who fought the 2009 EU Parliament campaign as my No.3 but who was sadly not elected) and myself.

Theresa May has voluntarily signed up to the EU Investigation Order, so that a Bulgarian prosecutor can demand your bank details or your DNA, and the British police are obliged to obtain these data and pass them to Bulgaria. No checks, no balances, no safeguards for the citizens (just as with the scandalous EU Arrest Warrant). The police are already protesting about the additional work-load at a time of major cut-backs. And what happened to data protection? This is a gross infringement of individual liberty – and the Coalition bought it without a fight.

Then there's the new EU regulatory structure for financial services. The City of London has the lion's share of the EU's financial services business, yet we've agreed for it to be regulated from Brussels and Frankfurt. Companies and high-net-worth individuals are already buying tickets to Switzerland in consequence. I pay credit to my colleague Vicky Ford MEP who has fought tooth-and-nail, and with some success, to modify the proposals and limit the damage. But we have conceded the principle, and that's a gross dereliction of the government's duty.

ABOVE: My stand in the Freedom Zone at the 2010 Conservative Party Conference with my staffers Joseph Bono, Neelam Cartmell and Lydia Smith. The Freedom Zone is organized by the Freedom Association and is rapidly establishing itself as the key fringe venue – some dare to say even the true party conference given the vast numbers of lobbyists, quangocrats and assorted hangers-on who are taking over the formal conference.

So what about the Referendum Lock? It is a meaningless piece of spin. They talk about referenda on new Treaties, but because of the passerelle clauses in the Lisbon Treaty, Brussels doesn't need new treaties. It can pursue "Ever Closer Union" within the existing Treaty framework. Our Referendum Lock plans refer to the ratchet clauses, but leave so many grey areas that, given the current attitude to Brussels, we can have little confidence in them. Not so much a Referendum Lock – more a stable door slammed when the horse is long gone.

Why are they doing this? Weren't Cameron and Hague of a broadly sceptic disposition? Well their first priority is, quite rightly, the deficit, and so their second priority is to keep the Coalition on an even keel to deal with the deficit. For these reasons they don't want to be distracted by a huge row with Brussels, nor do they want a huge row with the Lib-Dems.

But the underlying problem is that they regard Europe as a separate issue in a separate box, and moreover an issue way down the voters' priority list. It's something that happens "over there". They've failed to grasp the fundamental nature of this threat to our independence, our democracy and our liberty. Sometimes, I despair for my Country.

Nick Clegg wants "to narrow the gap between rich & poor". Tories want increased prosperity for everyone. That's the gap between us & them.

On 14 November I tweeted "The EU/Sovereignty Bill is transparently futile spin. It simply demonstrates the Tory Party's contempt for its eurosceptic wing". The tweet was picked up across the blogosphere, notably by Tim Montgomerie of the ConHome blog who retweeted it and so ensured it got a much wider audience. The response was huge, so I felt I had to explain what I meant on my blog.

The EU Bill, and the Referendum Lock

A couple of days back the Coalition published its EU Bill, which seeks to enshrine the so-called "Referendum Lock". This will provide for a UK referendum on new Treaties, and on new transfers of powers to Brussels under existing treaties. But (of course there's a "But"), this will apply only when Ministers consider that the powers concerned are sufficiently significant to warrant a referendum. In other words, we have a cast-iron guarantee of a referendum whenever Ministers think a referendum is necessary. But we scarcely

Today's the Day. Choose hope over fear. Vote early and vote Tory!

need that enshrined in law – it would happen anyway.

This is why I describe it as transparently futile. It is intended to confirm a promise – but it's no more than a promise to act if and when the government feels like it.

And we are right to have serious doubts about the government's willingness to act. With Angela Merkel's demand for a new Treaty on financial regulation of EU economies, we have the chance, as Mats Persson of Open Europe has pointed out, to negotiate. Cameron has some leverage, if only he chooses to use it. He can demand repatriation of powers, or opt-outs, in exchange for allowing Merkel to have her new financial oversight within the eurozone (and we must be clear: there must be no EU oversight outside the eurozone).

But William Hague has already answered this question: there will be no referendum on this issue. We are simply throwing away a strong hand of cards before the game begins. Europe Minister David Lidington has indicated that he expects no referendum in this parliament – perhaps for five years.

Yet as I have said several times, this government has been handing powers to Brussels arguably faster than the previous Labour administration. In a bare six month we've seen the EU diplomatic service; EU financial regulation: the EU Investigation Order;

votes for convicts in jail; and now the roll-over on the budget. This government has no business to ask us to trust it on Europe, and the EU Bill confers no new powers on parliament or on the people – in effect, it merely asks us to keep trusting the government, on an issue where it clearly has not earned our trust, and appears to have no intention of attempting to do so.

The Bill is merely intended as a sop to eurosceptics, to buy off opposition and rebellion. Yet for the government to offer a sop which is transparently worthless is, as I said in my Tweet, merely to demonstrate contempt for those to whom the sop is offered. And Cameron should never forget that the great majority of Conservative members and activists are eurosceptics. If they are to be treated in this cavalier fashion, it would be unwise to rely on their enthusiasm and commitment in future elections.

The leftward drift of the coalition continued and over Christmas 2010 I was alarmed to hear rumours that the coalition might be converted into a permanent alliance that would become a merger of the two parties. The rumours seemed to be emerging from sources very close to David Cameron. I pondered for a few days, then wrote an article for the ConHome blog on the subject. It was published on 3rd January 2011.

A Con-LibDem merger? I will not be a member of such a mongrel party

We all understand the reasons for the Con/Lib-Dem Coalition. Virtually no Conservative wanted it, but most of us recognised that it was the best we could do, given the electoral arithmetic. We understood the sacrifices and the compromises, but we admitted through gritted teeth that they were a price worth paying to see a Conservative Prime Minister in office, and even more important, to address the fiscal crisis.

The trouble is that it seems some Conservatives are getting just a bit too comfortable with it.

Cameron initially ruled out any Con/Lib-Dem pact in by-elections, or in the next General Election. More recently he has softened this position enormously with his "we have no plans" formulation. Meantime Conservative grandees who should know better have spoken up for a permanent electoral pact (like John Major -- did I really vote to select him for Huntingdon all those years ago? Fraid so!). And the word "merger" is heard rather too often.

We see this approach in the shameful and supine approach of the Conservative Party to the Oldham & Saddleworth by-election. My sympathy goes out to our candidate Kashif Ali, apparently running as a paper candidate to preserve the absurd fiction that "We fought this by-election as Conservatives". No we didn't. We have sent out the strongest possible signal that we are supporting the Lib-Dems, to save Nick Clegg's face. We have failed to campaign as Conservatives. It is widely reported, and not denied, that Andrew Mitchell argued to universal agreement, in Cabinet, that we should do everything possible to support the Lib-Dems.

But why? We all know the inter-party tactics and sensitivities, but we also know that whatever we do, the Lib-Dems will be crucified in Old & Sad, and will come a very poor third -- if not fourth. It is a racing certainty that Labour will win the seat, with Conservatives second. Labour will benefit from the opprobrium that always attaches to instigators of legal challenges resulting in by-elections; from a large-scale defection of Lib-Dem voters; and from their ten-point surge in the opinion polls since the election.

(Note that I was wrong here. Labour won alright, but it was the LibDems who came second and the Conservatives third, which did at least support my point that we fought a dismal campaign.)

There was just an outside chance that we Conservatives might have won it, if we'd made an effort, but no chance that the Lib-Dems would win under any circumstances. We've gifted Labour a seat that they might have lost.

But let's look beyond January 13th to the next General Election, which I expect will be fought under the traditional First-Past-The-Post system. I personally have been happy (and occasionally proud) to be a

Conservative Party member for decades, and a Conservative parliamentarian since 1999. But I have winced at times at some of the decisions the Party has made. The tax hikes. Ken Clarke's justice policies. Our obsession with climate change. And most of all, underlying the whole of politics like the drum-beat in Ravel's Bolero, the decades-long betrayal on Europe. On most of these issues, I sense that the Party rank-and-file is a great deal closer to my position than to that of the Conservative High Command (and MEP or not, I very much identify with the Party's rank-and-file).

And what do the Lib-Dems bring to the party? An even more limp-wristed approach to immigration, and justice. A positively dangerous attitude to terrorism, as we can see from the current debate on Control Orders. Their "Pupil Premium", which subsidises failure when we should be investing in success. A general pretension to fiscal probity, undermined at every point by a determination to spend on particular pet issues. A blind, lunatic obsession with the climate issue, and a closed-minded determination to spend eye-watering sums on futile attempts at mitigation. And above all, total subservience to the EU.

We shall never have a robust EU policy while we consort with Clegg and his kind. We shall never see the repatriation of powers from Brussels that we promised (and then forgot). We shall continue meekly passing authority and responsibility for our governance from Westminster to the EU.

I got into politics in the first place to oppose Britain's absorption into Europe. As The Lady Galadriel says in The Lord of the Rings, "Together through ages of the world we have fought the long defeat." Or at least, in my case, for a dozen years. I have not engaged in that fight for the whole of my political life to give up now, on the altar of short-term political expedience.

Today, with a new Westminster intake of mainly euro-sceptic young Conservative MPs, we have as good a chance as ever of making progress. Yet a Lib-Dem merger would throw that chance away.

So I give notice to anyone who may be interested: I will not be a member of such a mongrel party. I will not represent it in Brussels. I will not campaign for it, and I will not vote for it. And nor, I suspect, will most of the Conservatives I know.

OK, I was angry. But I think with reason. Things lurched from bad to worse. The EU Sovereignty Bill came before Parliament and proved to be every bit as supine as I had feared. It was no more than a paper tiger, designed to give the impression of a tough policy on the EU while making no difference whatever in the real world. It was a cynical ploy designed to give a spurious veneer of democratic legitimacy and accountability to a fundamentally anti-democratic process. The measure was designed to buy off dissent amongst Conservative Eurosceptics in the Commons, but it failed as feelings ran high.

On 14th January I wrote again for ConHome. The response to my earlier article had been large and I felt that some further words were needed.

If the Conservative Party has ceased to be conservative, what exactly is the point of it?

"If the salt hath lost its savour, wherewith shall it be salted?" Forgive me for starting off with a quote from the Good Book. Please just regard it as paying respect to the 400th Anniversary of the King James Version. But for those less than comfortable with the cadences of the seventeenth century, let me offer you a paraphrase in a modern context. If the Conservative Party has ceased to be conservative, what exactly is the point of it?

As the months go by, I've become increasingly concerned about aspects of Coalition policy, and making every allowance for the exigencies of coalition, I'm getting more concerned by the day. It's not just one or two policies. It's a broad range. I know there's some good stuff. Sorting the fiscal problem. Iain Duncan Smith on Welfare. Michael Gove on Education. But think of the bad stuff.

Ken Clarke's justice policies. Our decision to decimate the armed forces while they're still fighting and dying in Afghanistan (and I exonerate Liam Fox -- I expect he feels just as badly about it as I do).

I have written extensively on Europe, so I won't repeat it all. But the fact remains that we're handing new powers to Brussels faster than Labour did before us. We've failed to make a stand

ABOVE: At the Daily Telegraph party held at the 2010 Conservative Party Conference Emma McClarkin (my fellow Conservative MEP from the East Midlands from the 2009 election onward) and I were delighted to meet Boris Johnson.

twitter

"Cameron tried to stop the election of Bill Cash as Chairman of the EU Scrutiny Committee" (Sun. Tel.). I don't like the sound of this.

at any point. And now we have the effrontery to bring forward this "Sovereignty Bill", which is no more than pathetic window dressing. We whipped Conservative MPs to oppose an amendment that did no more than reassert the sovereignty of parliament. What were we thinking of? We're not fit to call ourselves Conservatives.

twitter 🐦

Shakespeare's take on the Lib-Con deal:
"If it were done, it were well it were
done quickly".

We have become obsessed by the
modish nonsense of climate change, yet
our policies, even in their own terms,
will have a trivial impact on climate.
But they will do huge damage to our
economy. They will drive a million
families into fuel poverty. They threaten
our energy security. And they will drive
energy-intensive industries, and
investment, and jobs, out of the UK
altogether -- and into remote
jurisdictions with lower environmental
standards. These are the very
manufacturing industries that Cameron
and Osborne are relying on to
"rebalance the economy".

But my biggest concern right now is
tax. There is the public backlash which
will result from our pig-headed
determination to implement the fuel
duty escalator, but that may be the least
of our problems. We are driving up
taxes on high earners to the point where
the damage to the City of London is
real and immediate, not merely
speculative and probable.

Yesterday's press carried an analysis
of the early impact of the "Non-Dom
Tax", a £30,000 levy, which was
simply a populist measure to "share the
pain". Since its introduction, the
number of non-doms in the UK has

fallen by 16,000, or 11%. The levy is
estimated to bring in £350 million in
2009/10. But the Treasury estimates
that non-doms as a category pay a total
of £7 billion a year in income and other
taxes in the UK. If we've lost 11%,
that's £770 million - more than double
the revenue. And that's without
counting the businesses and the skills
we've forced into exile.

This is a perfect example of a general
point that I make ad nauseam: raising
tax rates won't deliver a proportionate
rise in revenues, and may actually
reduce them.

Then there's Labour's 50% income
tax band, which we have failed to
cancel. It is already driving high
earners, and high-earning businesses,
out of London, to the benefit of
Switzerland and Frankfurt. Add to
that the Coalition's crass bank-bashing,
and it seems we have a death-wish for
the City of London.

Let me quote Jeremy Warner (in
another Biblical reference):

"We can cleanse the temple of the
money-changers if we like, but it won't
get rid of the money-changing. Some
other jurisdiction will end up with the
economic advantage instead".

Like many Conservatives, I am in
despair over the direction we are taking,
and the self-inflicted damage we are
doing. Where do we go from here? Is
anyone in Downing Street listening?

I began this chapter with a summary of the Reinstate Roger Row. My feeling then was that the Conservative High Command of the day were so keen to ingratiate themselves with our party's natural enemies (in that case the EPP) that they were willing to sell out on principles held dear by our party's members and voters. And in that instance it was I who got caught in the crossfire and was singled out for damage.

I close now with the feeling that the Conservative Party hierarchy is at it again. The High Command want to ingratiate themselves with the LibDems to keep the coalition in place and with the EU Commission to avoid a row with the EU. Once again Conservative principles are being betrayed.

"Plus ça change", as our EU friends might say.

BELOW: After the General Election of 2010 the Conservatives formed a coalition government with the Liberal Democrats. Ministerial positions were shared between the two parties, but I was pleased that the key post of Home Secretary went to a Conservative: Theresa May. Here my colleague as Conservative East Midlands MEP, Emma McClarkin, and I meet Theresa soon after her appointment.

It's the Economy, Stupid

I realise that some might feel that I have so far been rather guilty of introspection. The EU, the Euro and the internal machinations of the Conservative Party may be of burning and overwhelming interest to those of us caught up in the day to day struggles of the political moment, but they are of rather less interest to the public at large.

So let me turn now to a subject that cannot possibly be anything other than of great importance: The economy.

The financial crisis that engulfed the banking system had a profound effect out in Brussels. Here I thought I should concentrate more on events in Britain. Looking back I am rather ashamed to see that so far as my website and blog are concerned I was rather late to the issue – other than as it affected the Euro currency. I recall talking about it at some length in speeches and such, but I can't lay my hand on them right now. So let me kick off with an article on my website dating from 16th October 2008.

BELOW: The Derby Carriage and Wagon Works owned by Bombardier are a key industrial employer in the East Midlands, so I was keen to visit them and learn more about their works and plans for the future. I was shown about by Heidi Lee, Communications Manager for Bombardier.

Market failure? Or policy and regulatory failure?

The conventional wisdom is that the current financial crisis marks the failure of markets, possibly the end of capitalism. We have had Will Hutton doing the rounds of the media studios pouring scorn on anyone who has a good word for free markets. Even the very sound Roger Bootle of Capital Economics has been saying that perhaps banks are rather like public utilities, and need more government involvement.

So are we looking at market failure? Of course some institutions have behaved rashly. Of course the remuneration structures for bankers have encouraged short-termism. Of course (here comes the cliché!) lessons must be learned.

But this is not all down to the market. In many ways it reflects policy and regulation failure as much as, or more than, market failure. Which begs the question: if regulation is part of the problem, why do we think that more regulation is the solution?

Let me offer you four examples.

I have been struck by an article from 1999 by Steven A. Holmes, recently re-printed in the New York Times. He says quite explicitly that the Clinton Administration was pressuring Fannie Mae to relax lending criteria and increase housing loans to low and middle-income Americans, and minorities, who would otherwise not qualify. So at least to start with, the growth in sub-prime lending was not about spivs earning bonuses — it was the Democratic Administration's considered policy.

There can be little doubt that the US government was behind the relaxation of credit criteria, and therefore a major driver of the housing bubble that has caused all the problems. Policy failure, not market failure. It would be interesting to know if our fresh and dewy-eyed Labour government in the UK, casting admiring glances at the Clinton phenomenon, made any similar moves at that time.

Then there was Alan Greenspan. Like most people, I regarded him as a genius who had helped the world recover from the dot.com crash. I thought the US — and the world — economies were safe in his hands. Clearly Gordon Brown still thinks so. But with 20/20 hindsight, the truth is revealed. Greenspan was focussing on consumer price inflation, while letting asset price inflation rip. He believed that asset bubbles didn't matter. We know better now. So he kept US interest rates too low for too long, another major factor in the housing bubble that has come back to haunt us. You can't blame the bankers for that, any more than you can blame the fish for the water they swim in. Policy failure, not market failure.

Third example: marking to market. At first sight, the practice of valuing assets for accounting purposes at their actual market price on the day seems to be fair and proper and transparent. It prevents sharp bankers from over-valuing assets and presenting a false accounting picture. That's fine, however, while there is a market. When panic grips the market as it has recently, suddenly there is no market price. No one can sell anything. The mark-to-market rule means assets must be marked down close to zero, and institutions that would probably be viable in the medium term are bankrupt in the short term. Regulation was fine for the good times, but failed in a crisis. Not market failure — regulatory failure.

Then there was Northern Rock. In passing, recall that Gordon Brown constantly repeats the mantra that this was a crisis created in America, and exported to the world. The truth is different. The housing bubble in the UK developed broadly in parallel with the US, and the Northern Rock problem was home-grown. In the old days, when Britain was an independent country, the Bank of England would have called a meeting in marble halls with mahogany panelling, heads would have been banged together, Lloyds would have quietly taken over Northern Rock, and the whole affair would have been covered in one column on page seven of the FT. No panic. No queues outside the bank. No damage to the City and the country's reputation.

So what happened in 2007? The Bank of England was uncertain how EU rules, on transparency and state aid, applied. It was impossible to sort the problem in private. Panic ensued, with the first run on a UK bank for over a century. The fumbled response was a direct result of EU regulation. Not market failure: regulatory failure.

The markets did not cover themselves in glory. But much of the blame lies with central banks, policy-makers and regulators. Do not believe for a moment that the solution is more of the same.

A few weeks later, on 7th December, I turned to the role of Gordon Brown – then our Prime Minister – in the developing crisis.

The economic naiveté of Gordon Brown

For a man who acquired a certain reputation as a Chancellor, at least during the good times, Gordon Brown shows an extraordinary ignorance of economics.

He (and large sections of the media) urge the banks to pass on to borrowers in full the Bank of England's recent Base Rate cuts. There are two implicit assumptions here: first that this will put money in folks' pockets, get the tills ringing and rescue the economy from recession. Second, that the banks have a moral obligation to pass on the cuts, and are simply wicked profiteers if they fail to do so. Wrong on both counts.

Brown seems to have ignored the fact that lower rates for borrowers mean lower rates for savers. There are more savers than borrowers, and they tend to be older people. Older people may well depend on interest income to live on. They are also more likely to vote, and right now they are acutely worried about low interest rates on their savings. But if the extra pound in the pocket of borrowers is taken from the wallet of savers who relied on the income, we're looking at a more-or-less zero-sum game. Lower interest rates will not increase spending, nor boost the economy as Brown expects.

Nor is it obvious or morally right that the banks should pass on the full rate reduction. First of all, it was excessive lending and borrowing that got us into this mess to start with. There is no logic in asking the banks to be more responsible lenders, and in the same breath to tell them to lend at least as much as last year. Secondly, with the effective collapse of wholesale money markets, banks rely more than ever on retail depositors for funds. They compete in the market for savings. They need to offer attractive rates to savers, and that precludes them from offering aggressive cuts to borrowers. And to the extent that

banks can still borrow at all in the money markets, they are paying not Bank Rate, but Libor. On the day that Bank rate came down 1%, Libor fell only 0.3%.

Then consider that following the crisis of sub-prime mortgages and toxic debt, the banks, like it or not, have severely weakened balance sheets. It is in everyone's interests that the banks should strengthen their balance sheets. And the primary way to do that is to operate profitably, which is likely to mean operating on higher margins. Even where the government (and we tax-payers) hold large numbers of bank shares, the government has told the banks to operate commercially, and at arm's length. It is no good Gordon Brown hectoring and blaming them when they do what he told them, and make rational economic decisions.

With its ban on dividend payments in banks it has subsidised, the government, quite intentionally, has given the banks very strong incentives to pay back government funds as soon as possible, so as to be able to resume normal dividend payments (on which many of our pension funds depend). So the government has created an intentional and explicit objective for the banks to maximise profit — increasing the pressure to widen margins.

There is no possible point in the government creating incentives for the bank to behave in a certain way, and then kicking them when they do.

twitter

A deregulation plea, and a growth strategy: "We don't need to teach the grass to grow. We just have to get the rocks off the lawn".

twitter

Prince Charles: "It's cool to have less stuff". That'll help economic recovery, won't it? Glad I'm not a retailer!

But we can't expect economic wisdom and judgement from this government. Very soon they will be attacking retailers for failing to pass on their trivial VAT reduction. Of course they will fail to notice that the costs to many retailers of changing pricing and reprinting catalogues may well be greater than the VAT reduction itself.

As an MEP, of course, the management of the British economy was not among my responsibilities. What did come across my desk, however, was a string of economic measures produced by the EU Commission. Almost without exception these were bad for the economy, bad for business, bad for employment and just generally bad all round. A typical example prompted me to blog on 1 October 2009.

What a lot of cobblers

Mediterranean high end shoe manufacturers are trying to keep up the cost of ordinary leather shoes on UK high streets, to protect themselves from cheaper imports from China and Vietnam.

The so-called 'anti-dumping' measures currently in place, and being considered for extension by the EU, could see the tariff of 16.5 percent continuing on shoes from China, and 10 percent on shoes from Vietnam over the next two years.

UK consumers and local retailers would feel the brunt of the duties at a time when other household bills are rising sharply. Shoe prices in the UK could increase unnecessarily at a time when we are already facing higher household bills.

The EU is under pressure to further levy a tax on EU consumers in a vain attempt to protect Mediterranean shoe manufacturers who need to face up to the fact they cannot produce shoes more cheaply than Asian countries. China needs to be seen as an opportunity, but the EU is still treating it as a threat and trying to block it out.

Free trade is good for consumers and it creates more and better jobs. It may be painful for some, but the EU will gain in the long run. Burying our heads in the sand and pretending globalisation has never happened is the totally wrong approach.

The ways in which the EU Parliament works are varied and often weird. One rule is that you sit on a committee for two and a half years, then get moved to another just as you are getting into your stride. After the 2009 EU elections I was put on to the Employment Committee. I soon realised that most of the members were living on a different planet. By 1 June 2010 I couldn't bear it any longer and blogged accordingly.

The Madness of the
Unemployment Committee

I spent a truly surreal hour or two today in the European parliament's Unemployment Committee. On the basis that a problem shared is a problem dumped, let me tell you about it. The first measure we discussed was "Promoting Youth Access to the Labour Market etc etc etc". There was a long debate about whether unpaid internships should be made illegal, or whether they should be subjected to a maximum period of unpaid work, or whether unpaid internships should be conditional on the provision of some formal qualification or certificate at the end of the internship period. (Bear in mind that the European parliament is a hotbed of internships). There was a great deal more worthy pontificating about apprenticeships and traineeships.

Then we had a brief session on "Corporate Social Responsibility in International Trade Agreements", swiftly followed by "Remuneration of Directors of Listed Companies etc etc…". There was a sincere discussion of the maximum acceptable ratio between the highest-paid and lowest-paid employees; how much if any of total emoluments should be performance-related (i.e. bonuses); and whether bonuses should be short or long-term. We touched on the desirability of banning Golden Parachutes. We went on to "Atypical Contracts etc etc etc…", which seems to be an attempt to regulate temporary and freelance work out of

existence. This was followed by "Precarious Women Workers". Honest. I'm not making this up. I couldn't make it up. I presume that female trapeze artists would qualify as "Precarious Women Workers".

What I saw was a group of worthy-but-wet social liberal MEPs pontificating about employment matters, when they simply had no idea what they were talking about, and no way of assessing the potential impact of their proposals on unemployment, wage levels or economic growth. I doubt if any of them have so much as run a whelk stall.

Today we also had our new Europe Minister David Lidington in Brussels, and he shared with us his idea that the current recession should be the ideal opportunity to convince our EU partners of the need for radical labour law deregulation, for free and flexible labour markets. I agree 100% with David's objectives. They make perfect sense. But I am less sanguine about achieving them, because the mood of the Unemployment Committee is quite clear. They too feel we need an EU response to the recession, but their prescription is the exact opposite. Because jobs are under threat, they want higher social security spending and more "worker protection" (as they mendaciously call it). Tighten the regulatory screw. Make labour markets more rigid.

This perhaps illustrates why I use the term "Unemployment Committee". It

BELOW: I sit on the EU-South Korea Interparliamentary Group, which generally involves trying to establish good relations between the South Korean Parliament and that of the EU. Just occasionally we get to visit South Korea, as here in 2010.

also explains my belief that the European Union is beyond reform, and deserves to be put out of its misery.

The lunacy continued and there was no escape from it. In June 2010 I was out in Korea as part of the EU Interparliamentary Delegation when a document called "The G20 Agenda" was given to me. The G20 is a loosely structured meeting of finance ministers from the 20 countries with the largest economies. One such meeting was due to take place in Canada later that month and this document was the EU's considered views on what should be discussed and decided. I was so appalled, though sadly not surprised, by its contents that I fired off a reply to its authors.

Gentlemen:

Your short paper "The G20 Agenda" was circulated to the European parliament's Interparliamentary delegation to Korea, while we were in Seoul. I should like to take up a couple of points with you:

"Need to accelerate fiscal consolidation, but in a growth-friendly way". I think you have made a wholly unrealistic assumption that there are growth-friendly ways to cut spending and increase taxes. We know that this is not the case, and that any fiscal consolidation is likely to impact negatively on growth and economic activity. We have to do it, because our borrowing position is unsustainable, but

let's not pretend it's easy. To imply the opposite, without giving any practical examples of how it might be achieved, is simply to muddy the water.

"We should argue for ... structural reforms that can increase labour productivity". I am a member of the parliament's Unemployment Committee, and for years we have been passing a constant stream of measures designed to offer better "employee protection" (in fact these measures broadly have the opposite effect); to make labour markets less flexible, responsive and competitive; to increase unit labour costs in European economies; and to leave the EU less able to face the pressures of globalisation. This is the reality. This is the endemic culture which we have created in the EU. To argue now that we should push for increased labour productivity is to reverse decades of social and employment regulation.

I must admit that when I read it, I despaired. What is the point in talking about labour productivity (and preaching that message to the G20) when we persistently do the opposite?

I should be glad of your further comments.

Best regards

ROGER HELMER MEP

Answer came there none. Meanwhile the financial crisis was

plodding along. On 7th July I was moved to blog on the subject.

Random thoughts on the financial crisis

I don't usually comment in depth on the financial crisis, because the business pages are full of commentators who understand it a great deal better than I do. But I have a few points to make.

First, though, a caveat. This column does not take responsibility for financial advice. Indeed, would you trust financial advice from a politician in the first place? Investors should seek professional advice. Prices may go down as well as up, and the past is not necessarily a guide to the future (especially now). Terms and conditions apply.

To start with, let's challenge the conventional wisdom. "It's all the fault of the bankers". Or the hedge funds. Or the venture capitalists. No it's not. On the whole, the hedge funds and the venture capitalists do a good job. The banks have certainly been irresponsible, and have had perverse incentive structures, but they worked within the rules laid down by politicians, central bankers and regulators (Gordon

twitter

Is 20 weeks maternity leave (on full pay) good for women? More likely to make them unemployable. Another daft EU unemployment policy.

Brown's triple-headed regulatory structure didn't help).

It all started way back, with Jimmy Carter and Bill Clinton, good redistributive Democrats, who wanted to extend home ownership to disadvantaged folks who were unlikely to repay their mortgages. And they pressed America's big lenders, Fannie Mae and Freddie Mac, to do so, throwing out any idea of prudence on the way. Hence the infamous "Ninja" mortgages. Then the Central Bankers, starting with Alan Greenspan, kept interest rates way too low for way too long, arguing that asset bubbles would take care of themselves. They did, of course, eventually, and now we see the consequences.

OK. I admit it. I was a great fan of Greenspan. Now, with the benefit of 20/20 hindsight, I see the flaw in his logic.

Bizarrely, the rating agencies are also in the frame. Yes, they made the same false assumptions as everyone else. But they remain the canary in the mine, and there's no percentage in shooting the messenger.

So where are we now? The EU's massive Greek bail-out is under a cloud. The Germans hate it — and they'll have to pay for it. The funds may never materialise, and if they do, they may not be enough. They'd keep Greece out of hock for a year or two, but if they have to cover Portugal or Spain as well,

they'll soon run out. The Greek bail-out is contingent on an austerity programme which may prove politically undeliverable. Now we see suggestions that the fund could also bail out Europe's major banks. We've already spent it several times over, and we don't even have it in the bank yet.

Then there are the question marks over European banks, many of which have large holdings of government and other debt from … well, from Greece, and Portugal, and Spain. The EU is running stress tests on the banks. Results are due later in July. But it's already clear that they'll assume that government debt is good, because if they apply (say) a 30% haircut to dodgy sovereign debt, the banks will fail and confidence, what's left of it, will evaporate. So let's be clear: we're going to assume that everything will be OK, and this will lead to the conclusion that … everything is OK. Rubbish in, rubbish out.

Of course the left are correct to point out that significant cuts in government spending will have a negative impact on recovery and growth. But excessive government debt will spook the bond markets and drive interest rates sky-high — which will also impact recovery and growth. We are between the Scylla

Cadbury is to lose its 80-year-old "Glass & a Half" slogan -- because of EU metrication rules! You couldn't make it up.

of stimulus withdrawn, and the Charybdis of a sovereign debt crisis. We just have to hope that there is enough clear blue water between the rocks on either side to enable the Ship of State to navigate a middle way. In the UK, I think our coalition has it about right.

So where should you put your nest-egg (if you have a nest-egg)? The old assumption was that banks and building societies and government bonds were boring and low-return, but safe. We can't count on that any longer. House property has the advantage that bricks and mortar generally don't melt away (and you can live in your investment), and my own view is that there will be no further substantial falls in house prices. But I could be wrong.

One piece of good advice is to pay down debt. Another that still applies is to have a spread of investments, and not to put all your nest-eggs in one basket. More than one bank, more than one unit trust, maybe more than one currency and more than one national economy. Remember to take professional advice on which bank, which unit trust, which currency and which countries.

One of my very distinguished and well-known colleagues last night suggested — in all seriousness — that it was no longer daft to think of keeping a suitcase of cash under the bed. But which currency, and which bed?

During his long years as an opposition MP, Vince Cable had acquired a reputation for financial acumen. He had studied economics at Cambridge (I was in the year below him but our paths did not cross) and he then had a reasonably good career as an economics adviser to the Kenyan government and the Commonwealth Secretary General before in 1997 he was elected MP for Twickenham. During his years in Parliament, Cable made a number of statements and predictions about the economy. Some of these turned out to be accurate and he was lauded in the media (especially by the lefties at the BBC and Guardian) as a financial genius. Not all his prognostications had turned out to be accurate, but these were conveniently forgotten.

After the 2010 General Election, Cable went from being a LibDem enemy of ours to being Secretary of State for Business, Innovation and Skills in a Conservative-led government. On 30th September 2010 he came to Brussels and in his honour there was a joint meeting of the Conservative and LibDem delegations of MEPs. Next day I blogged on the event under the heading of "Vince Cable: Wise Old Owl or Headless Chicken?"

Yesterday in Brux we had (the first) joint meeting of the Conservative and Lib-Dem delegations, to hear from Business Secretary Vince Cable, perhaps the first Liberal Minister in the History of the World to speak in the European parliament. I'm still wondering why only half a dozen members turned up to hear him – but the room was full of staff, press, lobbyists and so on.

He delivered a very measured and reasonable speech about "Getting the European Economy Moving", in praise of trade and free markets. It was a far cry from his anti-capitalist rant at his recent Party Conference, and I even started to feel embarrassed for having passed round a handwritten note to Conservative colleagues "Vince Cable: Wise Old Owl becomes Headless Chicken". The note was seen by Lib Dem MEP Liz Lynne, and came back with "Disgraceful: you should be ashamed of yourself" scrawled on it.

Vince regretted the failure of the Doha World Trade Round (though seemed unaware of the considerable EU responsibility for the failure).

He recognised the serious damage that the Working Time Directive is causing, and called for its reform or repeal.

He was scathing about Brussels' plans to increase the EU budget by 6% at this time of austerity, when member-states, businesses and households are forced to cut back, saying quite rightly that the public would simply not understand the EU's failure to engage with economic reality.

So far I was nodding in agreement. But I had a series of questions I wanted to ask. Sadly, I had to leave soon after his speech, to catch a plane, so I was not able to do so. They were:

1 Given your support for a 50% income tax band, a mansion tax and a graduate tax, are you about getting the European economy moving, or stopping the British economy dead in its tracks?

2 As an economist, surely you have heard of the Laffer Curve. Would you agree with me that in Britain we are already on the wrong (high tax) side of the parabola?

3 Do you think that your stance at your Conference as a socialist ideologue was helpful to the Coalition? Or are you trying to isolate and marginalise yourself in the Cabinet?

Not everything in the garden was lovely, however. He spoke of the EU as an organisation "dedicated to free trade and open markets". Doesn't he know that it's a Customs Union with a common external tariff? How free and open is that? Doesn't he know that the CAP is inherently protectionist, and is causing massive damage to poor farmers in third world countries by denying them market access?

And he insisted that Brussels had been "pleasantly surprised" by the pro-EU stance of the Coalition, and assured his listeners that the new government was committed to positive engagement with the EU. I wish I could say that Vince had it wrong there, too. But I fear that on that point, he was spot on.

Climate Change Alarmists

If the economy is undoubtedly of great importance to the wider public, so too is Climate Change – or Global Warming as it used to be called before the globe stopped warming.

Long before I had started to take an interest in the climate issue, back in 2001, I remember seeing the famous "Hockey Stick Graph", which was the

BELOW: In May 2010 I went to the 4th Annual Heartland Foundation Climate Conference in Chicago. There I was delighted to meet Dr Fred Singer, one of the most outstanding critics of the IPCC-sponsored dogma that the current changes in the world's climate are caused by humans.

icon of the IPCC's Third Assessment Report (TAR). It purported to show that global temperatures for the last thousand years had been more or less constant, but had taken a sudden and alarming up-tick in the final decades of the twentieth century. It was a frightening image, and if it were true, it would certainly justify climate hysteria. But it has been shown to be one of the most misleading artefacts in the history of science.

I had difficulty understanding it at the time, as I had a rough idea of the main features of climate history over the period. Everyone agreed that the Mediaeval Warm Period took place AD 1000 – 1400, to be followed by the Little Ice Age in the 16th to 18th centuries. Everybody, that is, except Michael Mann, who had originated the Hockey

Stick Graph, with its straight line throughout that period. But this new version of climate history was seized on by the Warmists rather too uncritically. It agreed with their preconceptions, it justified their claims, so Hey, why argue?

Fortunately there were those who were prepared to argue. In particular, two statisticians Ross McKitrick and Steve Macintyre set out on a long and arduous campaign, first to reproduce Mann's results (they couldn't), and then to get Mann to release his raw data, and details of the statistical methods he had used to convert raw data into his all-too-neat graph. Both Mann and the academic institutions he worked for proved remarkably reluctant to help – though the tradition of science is that researchers share their data and methods freely for purposes of peer review.

As a former mathematician, I know very well that you don't prove a theorem by pulling a rabbit out of a hat and asking other mathematicians to believe you. On the contrary, you set out every logical detail of your reasoning from first principles to final conclusion, line-by-line, and you welcome challenges and new insights from other specialists. Only then can you write QED (Quod Erat Demonstrandum) at the end of your proof.

It's a long story, but Macintyre and McKitrick were finally vindicated, not least by a US Congressional Committee in 2006 under the Chairmanship of Ed Wegman, arguably the most prominent statistician in the US. And the problem is more one of statistics than of climatology. I don't know if Mann is a

> twitter🐦
>
> You couldn't make it up: Gov't to airlift fish from the Lake District to Scotland to protect against global warming

good climatologist or not, but the statistical techniques he applied to his data sets were fundamentally unsound. For those who would like to understand the murky detail of this long-running dispute, which is central to the climate debate, I recommend A.W. Montford's book "The Hockey Stick Illusion".

One of my first engagements in the climate debate came with an article I wrote in April 2007 for Conservative Home:

A different view on climate change

Is the earth getting warmer? Slightly.

Is there good evidence that the rate of warming is increasing and becoming catastrophic? No.

Is it caused by anthropogenic CO_2 emissions? Probably not.

Do proposed policy responses like Kyoto make sense? Definitely not.

Climate change hysteria has become an industry, with scientists, lobbyists and journalists making a good living from it. Many politicians are happy to connive, seeing opportunities both for higher "green" taxes, and for the global governance initiatives close to their hearts. David Milliband suggests re-branding the EU as "The Environmental Union", and adds for good measure that you can't be both green and Eurosceptic.

Worse yet, there are all sorts of pressures being put on the scientific community to fall in line behind the alarmist consensus. Counter-consensual papers aren't published. Their authors lose funding. Even work with only a tangential relevance to climate change can increase its chance of funding with the addition of the phrase "in the context of global warming".

I believe that the case for man-made climate change has not been made. The evidence over very long periods shows that while CO_2 levels are correlated with average temperatures, the CO_2 levels lag behind the temperature. The inescapable conclusion is that temperature drives CO_2, not vice versa.

Even if we accept the alarmist science, the measures proposed will do little to change matters. The effect of Kyoto, even if fully implemented, would be to reduce average global temperatures by $0.2°C$ by 2100 -- and less in the shorter term. We are being asked to decimate energy use, roll back the industrial revolution, and make heroic economic sacrifices, to achieve changes almost too small to measure. The resources that will be consumed by these endeavours could much more usefully be invested in a wide range of life-saving

humanitarian efforts as recommended by the Copenhagen Consensus.

Any CO_2 reduction programme which fails to engage China and India is doomed to failure in global terms, which is why America's environmental initiatives are likely to be more effective than the EU's. Incidentally, over recent years the USA's emissions trend has actually been better than the EU's, despite the latter's moral posturing.

I have accordingly organised a conference in the European parliament in Brussels to give a platform to scientists, economists, industrialists and politicians who broadly share these views. The Key-Note speaker is former Chancellor of the Exchequer Nigel Lawson (Lord Lawson of Blaby). The Conference will be followed at 5:00 p.m. by a screening of the Channel 4 documentary The Great Global Warming Swindle.

I have been asked how this plan sits with David Cameron's new green agenda. But the Conservative Party is a broad church, and it is right that these issues should be thoroughly discussed within a party context. I believe my conference can be seen as contributing to the party's new focus on green issues.

I also believe that there are profound reasons why we should nevertheless seek to achieve major reductions in the use of fossil fuels, but those reasons relate to long-term resource management, and to energy security, not to mis-placed global *climate alarmism. In this context, and while renewables have their place, there is no substitute for major new investment in nuclear capacity.*

In April 2008 I spoke on the subject of "Adapting to Climate Change in Europe" at a Plenary Session of the EU Parliament. As ever the EU Parliament was as keen as mustard to be seen to be doing something high profile and politically correct. I had no such ambitions, as I made clear.

Mr. President

I have four quick questions on climate change. Firstly, is global warming happening? Answer: no, the

ABOVE: Nuclear Energy represents the only serious way forward for power generation in the long term. Here I am meeting Keith Parker, Chief Executive of the Nuclear Industry Association to discuss the subject.

world has got slightly cooler over the last 10 years and the rate of cooling is accelerating.

Secondly, is it caused by mankind? Answer: no, there is increasing scientific evidence to show that what climate change we see is part of natural cycles and has very little or nothing to do with human activity.

Thirdly, can we make a difference? Even those who believe in global warming accept that the whole of the Kyoto process, if it were fully implemented – and it will not be – would make a tiny difference in 100 years time to global temperatures. All the efforts we are making will have practically no effect.

Fourthly, what will it do to our economies? It will be hugely damaging. As Mr Pęk rightly said, we are pouring truckloads of money into a doomed project and causing huge damage to ourselves, to European economies and to our children and grandchildren.

One month later I was back on my feet at the next Plenary Session on the same subject.

Mr. President

For once I come to the House with good news. Global warming has stopped. 1998 was the warmest year in living memory. For the last ten years, average temperatures have been flat or falling.

twitter🐦

"Peace in our time" was a delusion. So is Green Peace in our time.

The recent modest warming is comparable to what occurred in the Mediæval Warm Period, and before that in the Roman Optimum and the Holocene Optimum. Temperatures today are below the maxima of the last 2000 years.

Increasing doubts are emerging about the role of CO_2. Since 1850, average temperatures correlate well with solar cycles, but very poorly with atmospheric CO_2. The pattern of warming, both geographically and over time, is wholly different from that predicted by climate models.

The greenhouse models predict maximum warming in the high atmosphere. But observations show that most of the little warming we see is at the surface, and partly a result of the urban heat island effect.

The greenhouse effect of CO_2 is logarithmic, a law of diminishing returns. In greenhouse terms, the atmosphere is already saturated with CO_2, and further emissions will have very little effect.

Sea level is rising no faster than it always has -- about six to eight inches a century. Global ice mass is broadly constant. Severe weather events are no more frequent than they ever were.

Species extinction is driven not by climate, but by loss of habitat, and especially by the drive for biofuels. Recent studies show that polar bears are doing very well.

Climate hysteria is increasingly remote from reality. We need to rethink our policies before they do any more damage.

Of course the EU pushed ahead with its misguided policies, and I felt moved to explain in a ConHome article what the problems with those policies really were.

What's the worst way to cut CO_2 emissions?

Put ten economists in a room, and they'll come up with eleven different opinions. But there's one thing they'll agree on, and that is that taxes (if we must have taxes) should be clear, fair, predictable, easy to understand, cheap to collect, and above all, non-discriminatory. They should not distort markets and economic activity.

The EU takes a different view. It wants to limit CO_2 emissions by creating economic incentives. But its approaches break all the rules of good and fair taxation. Their first attempt was the EU Emissions Trading Scheme

twitter

BBC told to ensure balance on climate change. Will they comply? Will pigs fly?

twitter 🐦

The Guardian is having a go at my climate campaign. But as usual they're ignoring the message and taking aim at the messenger.

(ETS). *Phase One was a huge disaster. It was vastly bureaucratic and expensive to operate. It created serious distortions between member-states. And it wholly failed to reduce emissions. Open Europe has done a couple of excellent reviews of ETS's failure.*

Phase Two of the ETS started at the beginning of this year, which the EU says will be much better. But they've been saying that about the CFP for thirty years, so don't hold your breath.

One big problem with ETS is the initial allocation of permits, and "grandfather rights" for existing companies. These create huge anomalies. One of the most obvious can be illustrated by this scenario: Suppose two similar companies sit side-by-side, the only difference is that one invested a large amount of money five years ago on energy efficiency, while the other did not. If you allocate permits based on recent energy consumption, you are favouring the "bad" company and disadvantaging the "good" company. One possible solution is the auctioning of permits, but this brings problems of its own. Another anomaly is the cut-off threshold. One company may be caught in the scheme, while another slightly smaller escapes.

But a new idea is starting to emerge: Benchmarking. In simple terms, this means establishing a best-practice norm for emissions per unit of production in different industries. Then any firm that does better than the norm earns carbon credits, which it can sell to firms doing worse, thus creating incentives for both good and bad firms to improve. But of course someone has to decide on the norm for each industry. They need to update the norm every year as standards improve. They also need to identify those industries which in their nature use a high and irreducible amount of energy (like cement) and make special arrangements, to prevent them re-locating overseas (this is what is known as "carbon leakage" -- the ETS, like so many EU policies, tends to drive production and jobs and investment outside the EU altogether).

Then what do we do about new technologies which are not covered by the existing rules, or hybrid businesses that cover more than one category?

You can start to see the problem. We'll have a rule-book the size of a telephone directory. We'll have a vast department of bureaucrats setting levels by industry by year, and checking the performance of each company in the scheme. Every decision will be challenged by armies of industry lobbyists desperate to set norms and targets that give their own business a competitive advantage. Emissions costs will be unpredictable and volatile.

And the result will be massive complexity and endemic market distortion. So what's to be done? If you really want to reduce emissions (and readers of this blog will know that I am not keen to reduce CO_2 emissions, though I am concerned about energy security), the solution is a carbon tax. As a Jeffersonian in favour of low taxes and limited government, I hate new taxes with a passion. But a carbon tax would be vastly better than a false and artificial carbon credit market. It would be simple and predictable. It would be cheap to collect, with little administration. It would affect all businesses pro rata to their energy use, with no thresholds and cut-offs. And above all, it would create no anomalies and distortions.

So will the EU adopt that route? Will they hell! The EU generates complexity as a matter of principle. And emissions benchmarking will do huge damage to the competitiveness of European economies.

My continued snapping at the flanks of the Climate Change lobby must have been producing some sort of effect. So far, those calling with increasing stridency for financially crippling measures to be forced on the people of Europe had largely ignored me. That changed for the first time in the rather unexpected circumstances of the count for the EU Elections of 2009.

The leading candidate for the LibDems in the East Midlands was Bill Newton Dunn MEP. Now Bill and I have what is known as history. For years Bill had been a Conservative MEP, but in the candidate selections of 1998 I pipped him to the No.1 slot on the East Midlands slate of Conservative candidates after I made a robustly Eurosceptic speech at the selection meeting. I don't think Bill has ever forgiven me. After the 1999 EU Elections he found himself profoundly uncomfortable in a Conservative delegation that included Dan Hannan, Chris Heaton-Harris and myself. Not only did he defect, but he has since become something of a champion for climate change hysteria.

At the 2009 EU Elections, I was the No.1 Conservative candidate while Bill was the No.1 LibDem candidate. Not only did that put us head to head in the campaign, but it also meant that at the count we had the duty of making speeches on behalf of our parties after the results were announced. Since the Conservatives came first in the East Midlands, I spoke first. I thanked the officials for their work, assured listeners that the Conservative victory that night presaged the imminent death of Gordon Brown's Labour government and then passed the microphone. Bill spoke last because the LibDems had come fifth out of five in the East Midlands. The next day I wrote on my website about what happened next.

twitter

"Coldest May since 1996", says a newspaper report. It's Climate Change, folks, but not as we know it.

Sharp exchanges at East Midlands euro-count

The East Midlands European election count, at the Aylestone Leisure Centre in Leicester on Sunday, was marked by a sharp exchange between two of the re-elected MEPs, myself and Lib-Dem Bill Newton Dunn. Normally election counts are both formal and routine, and apart from the actual results themselves, unlikely to be newsworthy.

On this occasion however, Lib-Dem Newton Dunn chose to use his acceptance speech to claim that one of the newly re-elected members "denied climate change". He was referring to me, of course. I reacted to Newton Dunn's comments by interrupting "That's not true, and you know it". Newton Dunn repeated the accusation, prompting me to declare to the audience "There you have it -- a deliberate lie from the platform".

Now normally politicians are reluctant to accuse each other of lying, preferring softer phrases like "economical with the truth". But I think I was justified in my use of the word. Bill knows that what he said is just plain not true. It was a deliberate, copper-bottomed lie. In my leaflet published last year I had written "Everyone agrees that the Earth's climate is changing. Always has, always will", and to in my more recent Bruges Group book "Cool Thinking on Climate Change" I had written "Of course the climate changes. Constantly. If anyone denies climate change, they're just plain ignorant". The book includes a chapter that describes historical climate change in considerable detail, covering the long-term, medium term and short term.

Commenting on the spat for the press later I said "There is a real need now for politicians to regain the trust of the public. But they will not do so by telling deliberate lies in public. Bill has form on this. In 1998, he secured a well-paid job in politics by deliberately misleading his selection committee about his views on Europe".

Then came the astonishing events of "Climategate" in November 2009. A huge stash of climate data, emails and other documents originating at the Climate Research Unit (CRU) at the University of East Anglia (UEA) was posted on the internet. Despite a police investigation nobody has ever discovered if the documents were leaked by a CRU insider or stolen by an outside computer hacker. What the documents did make painfully obvious was that the supposedly magisterial, authoritative and impartial pronouncements of the CRU were in fact anything but. The documents contained numerous references to data being lost, fudged, corrupted or mislaid. There were also comments implying that the reports and studies released by the CRU had been

twitter

Ranting Greens on TV demanding higher petrol duty. They must be mad.

deliberately tampered with to give a misleadingly alarmist view of climate change. There were also suggestions that the leading climate scientists in the UK and USA had colluded to corrupt the peer review process that supposedly ensured high academic standards, and to destroy evidence subject to Freedom of Information Requests.

The outcry was great and the reputation of those scientists peddling the alarmist warmist line has never really recovered – nor does it deserve to. Instead of responding by being open and honest about their work, the warmist establishment has instead staged whitewash inquiries unworthy of the name, launched nasty personal attacks on those who dare to ask questions, issued a plethora of new reports as deeply flawed as those that preceded them and launched a massive propaganda drive assisted by their lefty journalist friends.

If they had only instead revealed their data and shown if it did support their conclusions there would have been no need for any of this. The fact that they have refused to do so only strengthens my suspicions that the data do not support their conclusions. In short, I smell a rat.

In January 2010, the Climategate data release was still new and not all the information had yet been studied. Enough was out, however, to show that something was very seriously wrong at the CRU. On 21st January I stood up to speak at the Plenary Session of the EU Parliament.

Mr. President

I have good news for the House. In common with many scientists, I personally have concluded that there is no Global Warming crisis. Global sea levels are not rising significantly. And as the IPCC has been forced to admit, Himalayan glaciers are not in rapid retreat.

The small increase in mean global temperatures over the last century is entirely consistent with well-established, long-term, natural climate cycles.

Copenhagen showed that many nations, especially China and India, are not prepared to sacrifice economic performance to solve an entirely speculative problem.

In Britain, a majority of voters no longer believe in man-made climate change, and they won't pay for futile and pointless attempts at mitigation.

The recent leaked CRU memos show that even the high priests of climate alarmism are in despair at the failure of nature to follow their forecasts, so they're falsifying the figures to sustain their fantasy.

We must now demand a full public enquiry into the suspect data before we spend a penny more on mitigation.

A few days later I wrote to the Daily Telegraph.

Letter to the Editor

Dear Sir,

The government wants to make substantial cuts to expenditure on higher education. Perhaps they could start by shutting down the Climate Research Unit at the University of East Anglia.

Yours faithfully

Roger Helmer
Conservative MEP for the East Midlands

And to the Independent.

Letter to the Editor

Dear Sir,

You report (Feb 7th) that Exxon-Mobil has given "hundreds of thousands of pounds" to climate sceptics. Yet you make no reference to the hundreds of millions of pounds expended by governments, local authorities, academic institutions, think-tanks and environmental foundations to promote climate alarmism. You seem unconcerned by the enormous earnings of people like Al Gore, and Dr. Ravendra Pachauri, Chairman of the IPCC, from the global warming industry.

Perhaps we should be grateful for a few dollars spent to give an airing to alternative views, before we crucify our

twitter

The mask slips: A senior IPCC figure argues that to solve Global Warming, we must abandon democracy

economy on the altar of environmentalism. What we are seeing is a confrontation between, on the one hand, the political, academic and media establishments, with enormous resources, pitted against the mass of ordinary people, and the still, small voice of common sense. And to judge by the opinion polls, common sense is winning.

Yours faithfully,

Roger Helmer MEP

One of the results of the Climategate affair was to galvanise the climate sceptic camp into action. In May 2010 the Heartland Institute in the USA organised an international conference in Chicago to showcase some of the peer-reviewed science that questioned the alarmist claims. I blogged from the conference as follows:

Consensus? What consensus?

I'm writing this in the Marriott Hotel in Chicago, where I'm attending the Heartland Institute Climate Conference (and I've just done an interview with BBC Environment Correspondent Roger Harrabin).

Ahead of the interview, I thought I'd just check out the Conference Speaker's list. There are 80 scheduled speakers, including distinguished scientists (like Richard Lindzen of MIT), policy wonks (like my good friend Chris Horner of CEI), enthusiasts and campaigners (like Anthony Watts of the wattsupwiththat.com web-site), and journalists (including our own inimitable James Delingpole).

Of the 80 speakers, I noticed that fully forty-five were qualified scientists from relevant disciplines, and from respected universities around the world — from the USA, Canada, Mexico, Russia, Sweden, Norway, UK, Australia and New Zealand.

All of them have reservations about climate alarmism, ranging from concerns that we are making vastly expensive public policy decisions based on science that is, to say the least, open to question, through to outright rejection of the Anthropogenic Global Warming (AGW) model.

Several of these scientists are members or former members of the IPCC Intergovernmental Panel on Climate Change.

But how do 45 sceptical scientists stack up, you may well ask, against the 2500 on the official IPCC panels? But of course there aren't 2500 relevant scientists on the IPCC panel. Many of them are not strictly scientists at all. Some are merely civil servants or environmental zealots. Some are economists — important to the debate

but not experts on the science. Others are scientists in unrelated disciplines. The Chairman of the IPCC Dr. Ravendra Pachuari, is a Railway Engineer.

And of the remaining minority who are indeed scientists in relevant subjects, some (like my good friend Prof Fred Singer) have explicitly rejected the IPCC's AGW theory. Whittle it down, and you end up with fifty or so true believers, most of whom are part of the 'Hockey Team' behind the infamous Hockey Stick graph, perhaps the most discredited artefact in the history of science. This is a small and incestuous group of scientists (including those at the CRU at the University of East Anglia). They work closely together, jealously protecting their source data, and they peer-review each other's work. This is the 'consensus' on which climate hysteria is based.

And there are scarcely more of them than are sceptical scientists at this Heartland Conference in Chicago, where I am blogging today. Never mind the dozens of other scientists here in Chicago, or the thousands who have signed petitions and written to governments opposing climate hysteria. Science is not decided by numbers, but if it were, there is the case to be made that the consensus is now on the sceptical side.

Meanwhile, the warmists were hitting back with insults, innuendo and a noticeable lack of hard science. On 23rd May I was driving over to the Brigstock horse trials (I'm a sponsor), when I put on the radio and heard Radio Four's "From Our Own Correspondent". I always enjoy that show, but I was riveted when Kate Adie announced that the third item would be on the Heartland Chicago Climate Conference. Of course I had just returned from that very event so I was interested to hear what the BBC had to say, especially as I had been interviewed by the BBC's Chief Environment Correspondent Roger Harrabin. Here was my take on the report as I blogged it later that day.

Maybe I'm biased, but I felt that Harrabin was seeking to debunk the whole event. He repeated the old canard that there is a "consensus", and that only a few scientists are sceptics – although there were probably more sceptical scientists at the Chicago Conference than there are committed Warmist scientists in relevant disciplines on the IPCC panel, and thousands of scientists around the world have protested at the so-called consensus. He described how the audience was baying for the blood of the University of East Anglia CRU scientists (you could hardly blame them in the circumstances), and were disappointed when their hero Steve MacKintyre (who helped to debunk the infamous "Hockey Stick" graph), urged a more conciliatory line.

We heard little of the surprising strength of the counter-consensus, or the widely-held view that the sceptics are winning the argument, and that only

those with a vested interest are still true believers.

But what annoyed me most was Harrabin's description of the Heartland Institute as "substantially funded by oil interests". In fact Joe Bast, the President of Heartland, had set out the funding position clearly. 85% of the Institute's funds come from private individuals and foundations (and not foundations backed by big oil). Only 15% comes from corporates, and of that no more that 5% from energy companies. None from big oil. In another piece earlier in the week, Harrabin had emphasised the point that some funding comes from the tobacco industry. This is smear and guilt by association – there is no reason to suppose that the tobacco industry takes a particular position on climate issues.

If Harrabin knows more about Heartland funding that its President has told us, then he should publish it. If not, perhaps he should apologise for the smear and innuendo.

One last point: James Delingpole of the Daily Telegraph spoke at the Conference. He mentioned that he is writing a book on the climate issue, and

twitter
Memo to Chris Huhne: "Britain leads the world in green policies". Yes. Like lemmings lead the world in jumping off cliffs.

twitter

News item: "Emissions cuts could still save the Polar Bear". But polar bears don't need saving. They're thriving. Doing just fine.

complaint. I wrote in the Introduction to this book that I was going to tell this story pretty much in contemporary words, not hide behind hindsight as politicians so often do, and here is a case in point. I put my hands up at the time, and here reproduce what I wrote then.

in the course of his research he has estimated the funding received by sceptics, and the funding received by Warmists (through research grants, wind farm subsidies, salaries of environmental journalists and council Climate Awareness Officers and so on). He estimates that the Warmist side receives around 3000 times more funding than the sceptics. Of course I can't confirm that figure exactly, but I have no doubt it's in the right ball-park.

Even big oil, which has virtually given up on funding sceptics, spends vastly more on green polices and green initiatives than on promoting climate scepticism. It is outrageous to suggest that those courageous scientists who dare to speak out against the Warmist agenda, risking their reputations, their careers, their access to learned reviews and academic appointments, are motivated by a few dollars they might have received years ago from the oil industry.

I continued my efforts to highlight the true nature of the science on climate change, and I flatter myself that I was being increasingly noticed, when I was brought up short in August 2010 by a

Sir John Houghton was Chairman of the Scientific Assessment Panel of the IPCC, 1988/2002, and he has a letter in today's Sunday Telegraph.

He complains that he has been widely misquoted. The alleged quote "Unless we announce disasters no one will listen" has appeared in numerous references over a number of years (try Googling it), but it seems that Sir John has only recently taken umbrage.

I have to put my hands up. I quoted him too, in my book "Cool Thinking on Climate Change", and I admit that the quote had been used so often, and apparently unchallenged, that I took it for granted and used it myself without going back to the source. Indeed I quoted the source used in another book. And when Sir John issued his denial, frankly I wasn't prepared to read the whole of his book from which the quote was claimed to come. It seemed easier simply to apologise. So I did.

Here the matter might have rested, but for two professors, John Adams and Philip Scott. Adams had retained a very full archive of materials on the climate debate. Stott runs an excellent blog. Adams discovered an interview

clipping from the Sunday Telegraph of Sept 10th 1995. Stott put it on his blog, at http://is.gd/8Rqqm. In it Sir John is quoted as saying "God tries to coax and woo, but he also uses disasters. Human sin may be involved; the effects would be the same. If we are to have a good environmental policy in the future, we will have to have a disaster". So let's be clear: Sir John believes that we need disasters to convince the public about climate change. He also seems to think that global warming is God's punishment for man's sin.

Sir John now protests that he said "If we want a good environmental policy in the future, we'll have to have a disaster". Indeed he did, though he doesn't repeat the very eccentric religious allusions, I notice.

So he denies the often-used quote, but admits to words that to all intents and purposes mean the same thing. We have here a distinction without a difference. So Sir John: I am happy to apologise for getting the detail wrong, but I absolutely withdraw any apology for the sense.

At the end of October 2010, I was invited to visit the CRU that had been at the centre of the climategate scandal. By this date the whitewash inquiries had concluded on the basis of very little evidence that there was nothing wrong, nobody had done anything wrong and that all was hunky dory. I had been invited following a correspondence with one of UEA's academic staff. A couple

of months before, I had asked if I could bring a couple of colleagues. They said yes.

The meeting did not go quite as planned, and the next day I blogged about the events.

A few weeks before my visit, the CRU asked for the names and any special dietary requirements of my guests (we were to have lunch while there). I replied Lord Monckton of Brenchley, and James Delingpole of the Daily Telegraph. For the next week or so I held my breath, fearing that they might not like to receive two prominent sceptics, but there was no further response. Not, at least, until a couple of days before the meeting, when I received an apologetic e-mail. They had just noticed who my proposed companions were.

Apparently protocol would not allow the VC to meet "political activists". If Lord Monckton and Delingpole had any questions, they were free to approach the UEA's Press Office. (In passing, I have to say it seems rather odd to describe Lord Monckton as a "political activist". An hereditary Peer of the Realm, a former adviser to Prime Minister Margaret Thatcher, a highly respected commentator on the climate issue, and Deputy Leader of the party that came in second place in the 2009 euro-elections. In any case, I like to regard myself, in my small way, as a political activist, and the VC was prepared to see me.)

I replied that this was deeply embarrassing to me, as I knew that Lord Monckton had made extensive (and expensive) changes to his travel schedule, between a financial conference in China and a business meeting in New York, specifically to attend the UEA meeting. In reply, they made an extraordinary proposal: Lord Monckton could not meet the VC with me, but he could have a separate meeting after my meeting was concluded. I decided to invite, on my own initiative, another MEP, Stuart Agnew (see back cover photo) of Eastern Region in place of Mr Delingpole. They could scarcely refuse another parliamentarian.

On arrival, I found Lord Monckton already there. Stuart Agnew and I were ushered into the VC's office, where we found the VC with three CRU professors – though not Phil Jones, nor the others whose names have become celebrated in the climategate saga. I immediately made one last appeal. It was absurd that Lord Monckton and I, who know each other well and have worked together on the very issue we had come to discuss, should have two separate meetings with the VC. But the VC was adamant: a joint meeting would create an unacceptable precedent. Monckton would have to come later. It was the VC's university, so I reluctantly accepted his dictum.

Then we got to the business of the leaked e-mails. At one point the VC referred to sceptics as "climate change deniers", and I pulled him up sharp. I

have yet to meet anyone who denies the plain fact that the climate changes. Indeed if the climate never changed, we should hardly need a word to describe it. The climate is only interesting because it changes.

Meantime the VC and his colleagues simply denied that any wrong-doing had taken place. The quotes which seemed to imply guilt were "selective", and had been "taken out of context". The VC relied heavily on the several academic/legalistic reviews of the scandal, in which the establishment has striven at all costs to justify the e-mails, to deny any guilt, and to protect the current climate orthodoxy. The VC insisted that if I had not read all of these reports (the thickness of a telephone directory) then I was in no position to comment.

But the quotes are quite clear. The "Hockey Team", which has a stranglehold on the IPCC process, and of which the UEA/CRU forms a key part, did indeed conspire to prevent the publication of dissenting opinions. They have indeed sought the dismissal of editors of learned journals whom they found insufficiently compliant, and too inclined to publish other views. They did indeed cobble together unrelated data sets (without explaining what they had done) to ensure that their "Hockey Stick Graph" complied with their expectations, and in order (in their words) to "hide the decline". They conspired to subvert the peer-review process.

The e-mails are explicit. They are the smoking gun. They cannot be justified by any amount of context.

As I said to the VC, if I catch someone with their hand in my back pocket removing my wallet, I shall conclude that they are a thief and a pick-pocket, and I shall be unimpressed if they tell me that I have taken their actions "out of context".

In a way I am reminded of a meeting earlier in the week, in Brussels, with three North Korean diplomats. They presented an entirely fanciful account of peace, freedom and prosperity in North Korea, and seemed uncomfortable when I explained that we knew, and they knew, that their description was nonsense, and hopelessly out-of touch with reality. But as we and they knew, they were obliged by reason of their positions and their employment to parrot the Party line. I fear that the UEA is under similar pressures.

The next great event for the alarmists was set to be the 2010 United Nations Climate Change Conference, to be held in Cancun, Mexico, from 29 November to 10 December 2010. I decided to go along – as did 25 other MEPs and 16 staffers – and before going spoke to the EU Parliament on the subject:

Mr President

Speaking in a personal capacity, let me remind colleagues that the public have lost faith in man-made global warming. Voters are sick of being blamed for climate change, and they're no longer prepared to pay for it.

More and more scientists are going public to challenge the climate orthodoxy. The credibility of the IPCC has been shot to pieces.

Recent small changes in climate are entirely consistent with well-established, long-term, natural climate cycles.

Copenhagen failed for the same reason that Cancun will fail. The USA with its new Republican majority in the House will not buy Cap'n'Trade. India and China will not forgo progress in the name of climate hysteria.

Our Green Policies are probably unnecessary, certainly ineffectual, and ruinously expensive. If Europe acts alone we will destroy our economies and impoverish our grandchildren while making no impact at all on climate.

We are embracing poverty by choice in the name of a disputed scientific theory. It's time to change course.

The line *Our Green Policies are probably unnecessary, certainly ineffectual, and ruinously expensive* was inserted deliberately. I had already booked a poster campaign across the East Midlands to highlight scientific uncertainties about climate change and they featured those words. As we shall see the poster campaign was to have unexpected results.

'Green' Climate Policies:
- Probably unnecessary
- Certainly ineffectual
- Ruinously expensive

www.rogerhelmer.com   European Conservatives and Reformists Group

JCDecaux

Meanwhile, I was busy blogging from Cancun.

Cancun, Dec 7th. There seems to be a fine tradition of cold weather developing around the successive UN climate conferences. In Poznan in 2008 we were shuffling through the snow to get to the event. I didn't go to Copenhagen in 2009, but I understand that exceptional cold caused serious problems. Of course we have no snow in Cancun, but delegates who expected 30 deg C and packed their tropical kit are looking distinctly chilly in the low twenties. Meantime in Mexico City overnight lows have reached an exceptional three degrees, and there have been reported deaths from hypothermia.

ABOVE: In November 2010 the IPCC held a vast meeting of climate warmist alarmists at Cancun in Mexico. I launched a poster campaign across the East Midlands to coincide with the event and to highlight my own views on the subject.

I have been predicting for quite a long time that Cancun would be about as successful as Copenhagen — in other words, it would fail. The sense here in Mexico is that everyone expects it to fail, so failure will be a non-event. Even EU President Rumpy Pumpy has said that the event is "heading for disaster", and for once I agree with him.

That said, of course any nugget of "good" news will be hyped and spun as a triumph. And they may get a few nuggets — especially in the areas of technology transfer and international carbon trading.

We already have the Clean Development Mechanism (CDM), which allows Western emitters to buy permits from less developed countries. This has been hugely counterproductive, with many of the permits bought from countries that would have reduced emissions anyway (like Russia, with the collapse of much of its old heavy industry); or outright fraud from countries that claim to have reduced emissions, and in extreme cases have created polluting plants so that we would pay to close them.

The third world is trading on the naivety of Western politicians and policy-makers. We've opened our wallets, and they're happy to take the money.

I am reminded of the mediaeval priests and monks who would flagellate themselves with whips to cleanse their sins, or the lay folk who bought Papal Indulgences to buy off years in Purgatory. Our transfers of millions of euros to third world countries (and Russia & China), and our "carbon offsetting", serve the same purpose — they give us a warm glow of self-righteousness while achieving nothing at all. But Hey, who cares, if the chattering classes feel vindicated?

Well I care, for one. We don't have billions of pounds/euros/dollars to blow on this nonsense, or on the hugely expensive and inefficient "renewables" we're promoting in Europe.

That's why I've launched my ad campaign "GREEN CLIMATE POLICIES: PROBABLY UNNECESSARY; CERTAINLY INEFFECTUAL; RUINOUSLY EXPENSIVE". Ironically, the poster campaign in the East Midlands has been delayed because it's too cold for the paste to stick on the billboards.

What wonderful irony! My regional billboard campaign was delayed – by the cold weather! While the Met Office was warning of global warming, it was so cold in the East Midlands that the paste wouldn't stick to the hoardings. It was the start of what was to prove to be the second coldest English December on record. Within a few days, however, with temperatures easing up to zero, it became possible to affix the posters, and they went up in Leicester, Northampton, Derby, Nottingham and Lincoln.

Back to blogging from Cancun.

Cancun, Dec 9th. Today was pretty much my last day at the Conference — I fly home tomorrow — so I was really keen to hear the up-date from Climate Commissioner Connie Hedegaard at five o'clock. Was there any progress?

The meeting took place in the Mais room of the Expo Centre in the Moon Palace Hotel (after we'd cleared out the previous meeting, which over-ran), and the Commissioner's first words set the tone. "There is not much to report". Later someone said, with a degree of cynicism, "It's been a pretty normal

Thursday", and Ms. Hedegaard added "A pretty normal COP Thursday".

Of course they may yet pull a rabbit out of the hat. Ideally, the event should finish tomorrow, but if they see any chance of the big prize, they could drag it out to Sunday. But the best guess is that the deadlock will remain on the main issue of a legally binding agreement, while the few nuggets I've already written about — forestry; technology transfer; a "Cancun Fund" — may be consolation prizes.

It still seems that only the EU (and a few smaller countries) really want a deal. But on the other hand, no one wants to be blamed for failure (except perhaps the US — it has a more grown-up attitude, and seems relaxed about taking the stick).

The Chinese are regarded as having played a good PR hand. At one point they issued a surprisingly accommodating press release, waited until they'd gleaned a good crop of headlines, and then quietly let it be known that there had been an error in translation, and their tough line remained.

The Guardian has made rather a fool of itself by hyping a week-old and very minor public document, failing to understand it, and sensationally claiming that the EU wanted to sink Kyoto. OK, so I don't trust the EU — but I trust the Guardian even less.

One bright point in the unrelenting green folly of Cancun. To my surprise, I found that one of the 215 exhibitors at the show was actually climate-sceptic. It was the US public policy organisation CFACT, who are good guys. I've written the odd piece for them.

And they were organising a meeting at the show. Top prize for courage, and taking the fight to the enemy. The speakers were Dr. Roy W. Spencer of the University of Huntsville, Alabama, and my old friend Lord (Christopher) Monckton, whom I had last seen on our joint visit to the University of East Anglia CRU a few weeks back.

I went to the meeting. It was a joy to find common sense in an unexpected place, and a bright note in the Cancun week. I have a great photo taken with two CFACT staffers, one dressed as the Earth Mother and the other as a polar bear — but sadly I can't download it till I get home.

Meanwhile, the poster campaign and my visit to Cancun had caught the eye of Guardian journalist Leo Hickman. It has long been a favoured tactic among the warmists to seek to discredit their critics rather than to debate the scientific issues – presumably on the grounds that they know they would lose. Now it was to be my turn for attempts to discredit.

Mr Hickman began bombarding my office with questions about who had paid for my posters, who had paid for my trip to Cancun, who had paid for this and who had paid for that. He also got very excited about my January 2011 speech to the Malaysian Palm Oil Council in Kuala Lumpur. He contacted others to ask their opinions of me, my views and my actions. At first I chose to ignore his provocations and to answer his queries accurately and politely. Sadly he did not respond in kind. In February 2011 I finally broke my silence and blogged about his actions.

Leo Hickman of the Guardian is a fearless environmental and investigative journalist, boldly shining the light of media scrutiny on matters where the public has a Right to Know. His most recent topic about which the public has the Right to Know seems to be the contents of my blog. He may have overlooked the fact that the public can read the content of my blog all by themselves, without his help, and many thousands do.

However, while my blog has taken years to reach 140,000 hits, I daresay that the Guardian website gets millions of hits a day, so thanks to Leo for taking me to a wider audience. Many politicians would kill for the kind of national media coverage that Leo is offering me. The trouble is that he is pursuing me with ever more detailed and vexatious questions, to many of which I simply don't know the answers (How much did my recent trip to Malaysia cost? I don't know, because my hosts paid for the ticket and the hotel, and I never saw the bill). If I blow my nose, Leo wants to know if the tax-payer bought the Kleenex

(I exaggerate, of course, but not much). He is also suggesting that he might write about me every week. If he does, then I'll really have to buy him lunch.

Fearless and dogged Leo may be, but he's none too accurate. His latest piece says "all his trips were … funded using his MEP's expenses allowance". But as I had told him, my Malaysia visit was wholly funded by my hosts, and previous trips to the USA were also part-funded by my hosts. But why let the facts spoil a good story?

His writing is not all kindly. He refers to my "propensity to court attention with his … alternative views". I didn't too much like that. But pity the poor politician. If he keeps his head down and gets on quietly, people say he's doing nothing and tells them nothing. But if he takes the trouble to inform them about the work that he does, and the issues on which he feels passionately, that's "a propensity to court attention". (And by the way, Leo, my "alternative views" on climate and Europe seem to be broadly shared by public opinion in the UK).

Leo's latest effusion runs to 1650 words. But if Leo isn't big on accuracy, he's not great on originality either. Much of his piece is quoted verbatim from my blog — so much, indeed, that I wonder whether I can apply for royalties. I'm saving the Guardian from paying for a whole lot of copy. In fact well over half his piece — about 920 words — is simply quotations.

It reminds me of the Mark Twain line: "Great blocks of quotations welded together with a thin mortar of originality".

But I'd like to turn the tables and put a couple of questions to Leo. One of them was posted as a comment on my web-site by a contributor called "Pimpernel", and I can do no better than to quote it verbatim: **Roger, Next time he calls ask him about the tax avoidance measures taken by the Guardian Media Group and whether he would like to make a comment about what the lost tax revenue could be spent on in these tough times.**

And I have another question for him. He was very excited about (and critical of) my visit to the Cancun Climate Conference in December. But I was only one of twenty-six MEPs (plus twelve officials and nineteen assistants) who travelled there at the parliament's expense. Is he asking the same questions of the others, including the British Labour MEP Linda McAvan, and prominent European Greens like Rebecca Harms (Germany) and Satu Hassi (Finland), who also went? And if not, why not?

I can save you the trouble of waiting for an answer, because we know what it is. For all his posturing about "tax-payers' money", he doesn't really give a hang about that. He has no problems if green MEPs go to Cancun to discuss ways of destroying capitalism and the Western world with lunatic green policies. That's all OK. He's getting at me because I dared to challenge the Guardian orthodoxy on climate. Simple as that. Leo, you're so transparent.

But you have to feel just a little bit sorry for the Warmists. They're losing the argument on the science. They've lost the battle for public opinion. There's really nothing left but to try to shoot the messenger — and they're all out of ammunition.

As I write this not much has changed in the climate change debate, despite much heat and fury. The alarmists continue to push out reports and make announcements of imminent disasters and mayhem, all on the flimsiest of evidence, then go on to demand ruinously expensive measures to counter these imagined dangers. Meanwhile, data are still hidden, workings out kept secret and methodology censored. Outrageous personal abuse is heaped on those who speak out against the establishment view, reports that produce awkward results are never published while their authors are stripped of funding. But little by little the truth is emerging. A few brave blogs publicise those reports, that the powerful and the influential try to suppress. More and more scientists proclaim the truth, even at the risk of their careers.

Oh yes, and no doubt Leo Hickman continues to grub through my travel receipts in the vain hope of finding something damning.

Has Political Correctness gone Mad?

If there is one thing that annoys my constituents who write to me more than any other subject, it is political correctness.

This pernicious construct of the self-righteous wing of the left-leaning intelligentsia has invaded almost every area of our lives. It is the sneering, holier-than-thou attitude of its practitioners that seems to rile people the most, almost as much as the ruthless intransigence with which its edicts are enforced despite the wishes of the public on whom they are foisted.

To be PC is to obsessed with not causing offence to anyone who agrees with you, but to be viciously abusive to those that disagree with you. Certain groups within society – ethnic minorities, greens, the poor, homosexuals, the disabled – are viewed as being beyond criticism, though they can be patronized in glaring fashion by those signed up to the PC agenda. Other groups – the English, the middle classes, heterosexuals, Christians, those who question climate change science – are fair game for abuse, insults and

---

twitter 🐦

Bizarre! The Women's Committee won't let the Unemployment Committee use the word "Women". Maybe they shouldn't use the word "Employment".

---

discriminatory laws. In short the PC doctrine is one of humorless hypocrisy.

Of course, the EU has vast budgets to pay for civil servants to continue to churn out this PC idiocy. They were at it in March 2009, as this press story makes clear.

EU's Political Correctness Attacked

Three Conservative MEPs have launched an assault on the EU's latest political correctness initiative.

Four weeks ago the European parliament introduced a guide to gender-neutral language, arguing that gender-specific language was "discriminatory". No reference can be made to a woman's marital status. Terms like "Mr. and Mrs", Monsieur and Madame, Signor and Signorita are out. MEPs must say "flight attendant", not stewardess; "fire-fighter", not fireman; business executive, not businessman. They are asked not even to say "man-made", but to use "synthetic" or "artificial" instead.

Now a group of MEPs, including Roger Helmer and Chris Heaton-Harris from the East Midlands, and Martin Callanan from the North East, have hit back, arguing that the EU claims to celebrate diversity, yet it can't even recognise the difference between men and women. They've tabled a "Written Declaration" in the parliament -- equivalent to an Early Day Motion in Westminster -- insisting that most people are comfortable to be one sex or the other, and expect their gender identity to be respected and recognised in forms of address.

The booklet insists that a person's sex "is or should be irrelevant in most circumstances". The MEPs argue on the contrary that a person's sex is fundamental to their sense of identity. It is an essential part of who they are, how they wish to be characterised, and how they relate to other people.

Speaking in Brussels, Helmer said "This is just another example of political correctness gone mad in the European parliament. It's time to make a stand for common sense". Heaton-Harris added "No one I know wants to be neuter and androgynous. They're happy to be women or men".

The MEPs have also demanded to know how much money was spent on the glossy booklet of unnecessary advice.

Then there were the little EU flags that suddenly started appearing on vehicle number plates about the time I was first elected as an MEP in 1999. In 1998 the EU Commission issued instructions demanding that all number plates had to conform to a specific design – and that design had to feature the EU flag. The instruction was not a law, however, merely yet another of those annoying demands. Many people objected to having an EU flag on their number plate, and opted instead for custom-made number plates that omitted it, or instead covered up the flag with stickers showing the Union Jack or the flag of St George.

A press story from November 2008 takes up the cause.

Recent news stories have reported that motorists displaying national flags on their number plates, instead of the EU flag, are being stopped and fined by police, and that cars going for their MOT tests are being failed because of "illegal number plates". Many motorists choose to display the Union Jack, or the national flags of England, Scotland or Wales in preference to the EU stars.

East Midlands MEP Roger Helmer had believed that the use of national flags was accepted (he displays a Union Jack on his own number plate), and he immediately wrote to Transport Minister Jim Murphy to ask for clarification, and to demand that the rules should be changed if national flags were in fact illegal. Within days, the government has announced that the national flags will be permitted. It is not clear whether motorists who have been fined will be able to reclaim their money.

Welcoming the government's change of heart, Mr. Helmer said "I don't know if my letter influenced the government's decision, but I am delighted that we seem to have won a small argument in favour of freedom of choice and national identity -- a small blow against European harmonisation".

I have also campaigned against the enforced use of metric mesurements. In 2008 I welcomed the British government's decision to advise councils not to prosecute traders for selling goods in Imperial measures. But I was concerned that the law is still on the statute book, and that traders selling a pound of potatoes were still committing a criminal offence, even though they may not have been prosecuted.

I was quoted in a press story as follows:

> Conservative MEP Roger Helmer says "We've only won half the battle. It's good that traders can keep using pounds and ounces without fear of prosecution. But it brings the law into disrepute when we have a clear law on the statute book, which is then set aside by executive discretion. The EU must now amend the relevant directive, and the British government must amend the UK law accordingly".

It is not only attacking PC nuttiness. Sometimes it is a case of supporting a cause that in an idealized PC world would be banned entirely. Like supporting our armed forces. In 2010 I was delighted to back Armed Forces Day with a press release.

---

twitter

Stella McCartney and PETA want the Guards to wear faux-fur bearskins. And maybe plastic belts and boots?

Armed Forces Day gets MEPs' backing

Armed Forces Day is an annual opportunity for communities and businesses to show their support for the men and women who make up our forces and this year's on Saturday 26th June has the backing of both local Conservative MEPs. The Duchess of Rutland held a fund-raiser for the Colonel's Fund with the Grenadier Guards and Roger Helmer MEP was delighted to attend and show his support (see picture).

With the ongoing military effort in Afghanistan as well as the constant work by our forces to promote peace, deliver aid and provide security for our nation I was delighted to support the fundraiser for the Grenadier Guards last Sunday just in time for Armed Forces Day on Saturday.

Other disputes are at first glance frivolous, but underlying issues are just as serious. Take the recent disputes over the wearing of the burka by some Islamic women. One Conservative MP, Philip Hollobone, said he would not welcome anyone to his surgery who covered their face. Another Conservative MP, Damian Green responded by saying that a ban on the burka would be "un-British".

My blog on the subject in the summer of 2010 ran as follows:

> *As an instinctive libertarian, I must admit that my first thought was to oppose any ban on the burka. We want*

88

ABOVE: In June 2010 I attended a fundraiser for a military charity kindly hosted by Her Grace the Duchess of Rutland. While there I met these two splendid fellows from the Grenadier Guards.

the government off our backs, not telling us what to wear.

But the libertarian argument works both ways. There certainly are Muslim women who choose voluntarily to wear the burka, perhaps as an expression of identity, or of faith, or perhaps out of a misplaced sense of modesty. On the other hand there is good evidence that many Muslim women wear the burka involuntarily, because of cultural, or religious, or peer pressure, or indeed because they are forced to do so by their husbands or other male relatives. So a burka ban would be an imposition on the first group, but would liberate the second.

We already accept social or legal constraints on dress in many circumstances. No one, I suspect, man or woman, would choose to enter a church, or a mosque, or indeed a court of law, stripped to the waist. Even if some new religion emerged which held it to be a religious duty to go bare-chested,

125

such people would not be welcome, or allowed, in churches.

I have often visited mosques and Hindu temples, and have been perfectly happy to take off my shoes. I don't see that as a restriction of my right to choose my own footwear. It is merely a courtesy to my hosts. Back in 1984, I visited the Temple of the Tooth in Kandy, Ceylon. I was wearing typical Englishman-Abroad baggy shorts, which I considered perfectly modest, but I was required to rent a sarong to wear over my shorts and bare calves before I was allowed to go in. Again, I had no problem with that – indeed I rather admired the entrepreneurial spirit of local people who had parleyed Buddhist modesty into a nice little earner, renting sarongs to the tourists.

And clothing standards apply more widely than in religious buildings. I believe it is still acceptable for women to go topless on Mediterranean beaches, but I read that local supermarkets are now insisting that they cover up in the aisles. Here in the UK, Tesco has banned customers wearing pyjamas – and quite right too, in my view.

We allow nudism only under highly restricted circumstances. Nudists may go naked in private clubs, or in specially demarcated sections of the beach. But let them walk down Oxford Street in the buff, and they will be arrested, and I should think that most Muslims would approve of that.

So we already accept the principle of social and legal constraints on our freedom to dress as we choose, in many contexts. The remaining question is whether or not such standards should apply to the burka. I think they should.

So we should say to our Muslim fellow citizens "You are welcome among us. You are welcome to live in our country and to follow your faith. But the covering of the face amounts to a public affront, a deliberate discourtesy to your host nation. Please don't do it".

On the BBC Radio 4 Sunday programme this morning, a Muslim woman opposing a burka ban was asked "What would you do if the burka were banned in the UK?" She replied that she would leave Britain and go somewhere more in tune with her faith and her values. I think that was exactly the right response. If you want to be part of our society, you are welcome. If you want to live among us but openly reject all we stand for, maybe both you and we would be happier if you went elsewhere.

Of all PC nonsense, the mantra of "human rights" is perhaps the most dangerous. As I explained in a blog of 19 December 2010, it could end up with people dead.

twitter

BBC weather forecast warns of 50mm of rain. If they mean two inches, why not say so?

twitter

Benjamin Franklin: "Beer is proof that God loves us, and wants us to be happy".

Are our judges deliberately perverse? Or does it just seem that way?

We face a situation where there is almost nothing that the government and the security services can do about known terrorist suspects, in cases where there is insufficient evidence to mount a full-scale prosecution. Again and again, our courts strike down attempts to repatriate them ("they might be mistreated in their own countries"); or to use any kind of preventative custody; or to impose curfews and to restrict their movements.

Again and again, the decisions of the courts are inspired by an extreme left-wing libertarian interpretation of the law, based on the extremely wide-ranging and ill-defined "rights" contained in the European Convention of Human Rights. And the decisions appear to imply an assumption that the rights of foreigners always trump the rights of Brits.

Before the General Election, the Conservative Party appeared to be committed either to the wholesale repeal of Labour's ill-judged accession to the ECHR, or at least to the creation of exceptions and derogations that would have allowed us to protect British citizens and to repatriate foreign

nationals whose presence in the UK was deemed a threat to public safety. There was loose talk of creating a new, British Bill of Rights which would replace the ECHR in this country. Personally, I never rated this idea. I rather agree with Margaret Thatcher that in this country we have democracy, and common law, and a free press, and that is enough – or at least it would be, if our judges exercised a little common sense, and were prepared to take into account the rights of British citizens as well as the rights of foreign terrorists.

In any case, the commitment to repeal the ECHR in this country, like so much else, seems to have fallen foul of the Coalition Agreement and Nick Clegg's knee-jerk approval of any EU measure, however ill-conceived.

On the back of all this we now have the case of Aso Mohammed Ibrahim, a 33-year-old Iraqi Kurd allowed to stay despite having killed a child, Amy Houston in Darwen, Lancs in 2003. At the time he was driving while disqualified, and he failed to stop after the accident. Yet the Immigration and Asylum Chamber has ruled that he may stay. They don't even have the poor fig-leaf of claiming that his life would be at risk in Iraq. They base their decision on his right to "family life". So what about the rights of the Houston family? No tribunal ruling can bring their daughter back. This man is exactly the sort of criminal alien who should be deported after serving his sentence, and if he wanted a right to *family life, he should have thought of that before driving dangerously while disqualified.*

If he is so desperate to spend time with his family, there is no reason they should not accompany him back to Iraq.

Both David Cameron and Immigration Minister Damian Green have expressed their anger, and called for an appeal by the Border Agency against the decision. And quite right too. But it's not enough. We need to fulfil our election pledge to draw the teeth of the ECHR. And we have to re-educate our judges. We have to find a way – heaven knows how but that's what the government is for – to establish a proper balance between the rights of British nationals and the rights of others. And (whisper it quietly), where these rights conflict, British judges must put their compatriots' interests first.

Of course, we can always rely on the EU to indulge in some ridiculous PC nonsense. They rarely disappoint. The following press story from January 2011 says it all really.

EU cancels Christmas, sparking MEPs' protest

Roger Helmer, an East Midlands Conservative MEP, has voiced his outrage at the EU Commission's decision to distribute 3 million diaries featuring the feast days of many faiths, but with no reference to Christmas -- or

twitter

Votes for convicts? Government says it has "no option". Fact is, it has no backbone. An outrageous response. It should just say no.

any other Christian festival. The diaries have been sent as a "gift" from the Commission to young citizens in schools across Europe. Information accompanying the diary details facts about the EU, and also the festivals of Islam, Sikhism and Hinduism -- but no Christmas or Easter. But predictably, 'Europe Day' on May 9 also gets a mention.

The reported cost of the EU diaries is £4.4m of taxpayers' money. A majority of EU citizens class themselves as Christians of varying denominations.

Mr. Helmer has joined with other MEPs in the parliament to co-sign a "Written Question" to the Commission, demanding an explanation, and calling on it to withdraw these diaries which fail to respect Europe's cultural heritage, and to take steps to ensure that no such mistakes occur again.

Commenting from Strasbourg, Mr. Helmer said:

"The key role of Christianity in Europe's history and culture is an undeniable and historical fact. Christian holidays, in particular Christmas and Easter, which are absent in this diary, are celebrated throughout all Europe by most citizens, even

including many who would not class themselves as Christians at all. It is simply scandalous that all Christian references were omitted from this publication. I personally doubt whether the omission was intentional, but it seems to reveal an instinctive anti-Christian, pro-minority-religion bias in the institution"

Talking of Christianity, a news story in March 2011 prompted me to hurl a bull into a china shop by writing the following letter to the Daily Telegraph.

Dear Sir,

I write to express my support for Owen and Eunice Johns, a Derby couple who have been denied the right to foster a child because they are committed to a traditional Christian view of morality. I greatly regret the perverse decision of the High Court, which has ruled that homosexual rights should take precedence over Christian moral values. No one is questioning the right of homosexuals to pursue their own life-style -- but why don't Christians enjoy the same privilege?

Not only have the Johns been denied the right to foster, but a needy child has been denied a secure and loving home. The Johns are denied the right to hold

views which until recently were almost universal, and are still widely held. Yet in these politically correct times, we are intimidated by strident minority lobbyists, and we are not allowed to express reasonable opinions.

We talk about celebrating diversity and supporting minority rights, yet we are prepared to ride rough-shod over the rights of decent Christian people to hold a conventional view of morality. It is time to fight back against this fanatical political correctness.

Yours faithfully

Roger Helmer MEP

The advocates of political correctness are ever eager to ban things with which they disagree. It is not enough that they stop doing something that they find disagreeable, they have to stop all the rest of us from doing it as well.

Hunting is a case in point. The East Midlands is the heart and soul of English fox-hunting country, with many of the oldest and best-known hunts across the six counties. Melton Mowbray in Leicestershire is absolutely the centre of the sport. The East Midlands also has a higher portion of agriculture than the national average, and country sports are clearly of interest to the agricultural community.

While we wait for the repeal of the discredited Hunting Act (at one point I almost had the champagne on ice), I continue to support not only the hunts, soldiering on successfully in the teeth of

twitter
I hate litter. But a 70-year old woman fined £2500 for dropping cigarette ASH at a bus stop? Outrageous.

the absurd Act, but also other rural pursuits. So I am delighted to be able to co-sponsor the Knaptoft Horse Trials, which take place in later July or early August in Leicestershire, with the kind permission of landowners Kim and Neville Hall. And Yes (before anybody asks) the money for the sponsorship came from my MEP Information Fund allowance. Bear in mind that all EU money is essentially our money. I am delighted if I can ensure that a little of it is spent promoting country sports in the East Midlands, rather than promoting European integration in Brussels.

In the summer of 2009 came the Parliamentary By-Election in Norwich, where a Conservative victory proved to be a harbinger of David Cameron's elevation as Prime Minister. I went to help our excellent candidate, and one aspect of Labour's campaign caught my eye. I blogged about it on my return to the East Midlands.

"Vote Labour or the fox gets it"

Rather belatedly, I picked up the story of a Labour flyer at the recent Norwich North by-election. The slogan read "Vote Labour or the fox gets it", and it argued the case that animal lovers should vote Labour to prevent a future Conservative government re-instating fox hunting.

"The fox gets it", says the slogan, but it's very clear that the animal rights lobby, and the Labour Party, don't get it. Leave aside for a moment the fact that the Act is unworkable, that

twitter

So the po-faced Miliband brothers "would rather have a Prius than a Jaguar". They're welcome to it.

something very like traditional hunting continues, that many hunts are going from strength to strength with increasing membership and support. Leave aside the fact that the Hunting Act was about class warfare and class prejudice ("Getting our own back for the miners"), not about animal welfare.

The fact is that the Hunting Act is bad for the countryside, bad for bio-diversity, bad for the environment, bad for the rural economy. But most of all, it is bad for foxes. Foxes continue to be culled and killed, and the anti-hunt lobby don't or won't recognise that all other culling methods threaten the fox with a slow death in a ditch from gangrene or starvation. There are no hospices for foxes.

Hunting with hounds is the only culling method that can guarantee either that the fox gets clean away, unscathed, or that it dies in seconds in a rush of adrenaline.

Hunting is also the only ecologically selective culling method, that preferentially takes out old or sick foxes, and so promotes the general health of the fox population.

Labour's Norwich North flyer is typical of Labour's approach to politics.

A snappy slogan, beautifully spun. And a total failure to engage with the real world or the real issues — especially with countryside issues.

For many years I've been in the habit of attending the Fernie Hunt's Boxing day meet at Great Bowden, near Market Harborough, and 2009 was no exception. The sun shone from a clear blue sky, and some hundreds of people gathered on the village green, with the riders and hounds. A thaw was just setting in, although I suspect not soon enough to allow serious hunting. But the tradition of the Boxing Day Meet was maintained. Mulled wine, coffee and hot chocolate were available from the Shoulder of Mutton on the green.

I remember thinking how strange it was that historic dividing lines between the generations are becoming blurred in the 21st century. For the first time in my life, I saw a man with an ear-ring and a hearing aid, in the same ear.

On my return home that evening I blogged:

The enthusiastic crowd at this event, and at a couple of hundred Meets up and down the country, serve as a standing rebuke to the envious and embittered kill-joys of the Labour Party, determined to maintain their Hunting Act as long as they can. Yet this was the day that Environment Minister Hilary Benn chose to launch an attack on what he called the Tory pledge to repeal the Act (of course we are pledged to a free vote in the House of Commons, not to repeal per se).

It is odd to reflect that Labour's tactic is based on a misconception. On the evidence of today's crowd at Great Bowden, I'd say that ordinary folk were better represented there than the chinless wonders and county squirearchy. Many hunt followers find it challenging to pay for their winter feed, but they hang in there because they love the sport, they love their horses, they love the countryside and they love the living tradition of hunting. I used to be an enthusiast for hare coursing before the wretched Act outlawed it, and while some of the owners were well-heeled, the crowd at the Waterloo Cup was always predominantly working class. Hare coursing has traditionally been popular with pitmen, so it is ironical that Labour's leftist ideologues imagine that banning coursing is somehow compensation for the miners.

It is not only with foxes that the lefties get themselves muddled and end up being counterproductive. In January 2010 the EU Parliament had a CITES (Convention on the Trade in Endangered Species) meeting, and lobbyists have descended in droves, including the serried ranks of IFAW and WWF. The touchstone question was, how do we save the elephant? Although very similar considerations apply to other species, not least the polar bear.

twitter

Jeremy Hunt is vilified for daring to suggest that parents should take responsibility for their children. What are we coming to?

At the time I blogged:

Across the parliament we see the hideous regiment of assorted socialists and lefties and greens, the bunny-huggers and the bleeding-hearts, who have a simple solution. Ban the ivory trade, and save the elephant. It appeals to the softer sentiments in all of us.

But socialism and sentiment are simplistic. They fail to account for incentives and human motivation. If you're a dirt-poor third-world farmer, and you've spent six months growing the very modest crop that you hope will sustain your family until the next harvest, you're not very sympathetic to an elephant that decides it has a prior claim on the crop. So the best strategy for that farmer is to shoot the elephant,

ABOVE: I am proud to support various country sports events, including the Fernie Hunt Team Chase, where I posed with my banner in March 2010.

and then sell the ivory on the black market. That's a win-win deal for the farmer, but a death-knell for elephants.

A better way is to make the elephant a sustainable resource, and to give the farmer a real incentive to tolerate the elephants, who in some parts of Africa are encroaching on agricultural land quite severely (indeed in parts of Africa, elephant numbers have exceeded sustainability, but that's another story). The plan is to allow a limited and controlled trade in ivory, but to use the proceeds to provide an insurance fund against which farmers can claim for elephant damage.

That removes the incentive for farmers to kill elephants to defend their crops, and potentially provides a source of revenue for local people which gives them an interest in sustaining the elephant population. That, at any rate, is the view of the Namibian and Tourism Minister, and I am convinced that she is sincerely concerned for the elephants, not merely looking for a quick profit by selling ivory.

Over the spring and summer of 2010 I attended a number of country sports events. Of the Fernie Hunt Team Chase in March I blogged:

For those unfamiliar with Team Chasing, it's a cross-country horse race in which teams of four riders compete against the clock, and against the other teams. They are measured not on the first man (or woman) across the line, nor on an average time, but on the time of the third rider. This allows each team to lose one horse on the way round — and given the size of the fences, it's perhaps a surprise that so many make it round. But it also puts a premium on team-work. There's no point in a star rider coming in minutes before the rest of the team.

The Tur Langton course (hat-tip to Sally O'Sullivan of O'Sullivan Farms, who generously makes the land available) forms a natural amphitheatre, providing spectators with a wonderful view. One can see most of the thirty fences from the car-park. I sponsored the 21st fence, "Helmer's High Jump", which was appropriately

challenging; and also the Foot-Race — a fun event over part of the course, slipped in at lunch-time between the main Team Chase races.

It was a cold and windy March day, but the rain held off and we even had a fair bit of sunshine. A great day for walking the course. The event illustrates a point often made by supporters of hunting, that the hunts are at the centre of much rural social life, whether the Hunt Ball, the farmer's dinner, the point-to-point, or the famous Fernie cabaret evenings. Couldn't you do all those things without, ahem, actually hunting foxes, ask the antis? Well yes you could. Just as you could have church socials and coffee mornings and whist drives and the Mothers' Union without actually having the Sunday Service, but what would be the point?

In September I congratulated Alice Barnard, former Regional Director of the Countryside Alliance covering the East Midlands, on her elevation to the position of Chief Executive. As an internal candidate, she saw off tough competition for the top job from several well-qualified outsiders.

I've known Alice for some years, seeing her most often on Countryside Alliance stands at country shows up and

---

twitter

The Pope says "Bring back Christmas". Bravo! I agree. But please -- no mince pies in September!

down the region. She's a very effective manager with a huge commitment to the Country Sports and to the Alliance's objectives — including the repeal of the Hunting Act. She has also been on the Conservative Party's candidate list.

By December of 2010, however, I was beginning to wonder how the new coalition government was getting on with repealing the Hunting Act. Like others, I had heard nothing. I blogged after again attending the Fernie Hunt Boxing Day Meet.

Today Sara (my wife) and I went to the Fernie Hunt Meet at Great Bowden. This is the traditional Boxing Day event, but the Hunt doesn't meet on a Sunday, so the event was held over until the 27th.

It wasn't possible to hunt, because the frozen weather has left the ground hard as a rock. But the Boxing Day Meet is such a fixture in the local calendar that it went ahead anyway. I was rather glad that no one asked me about the Conservative Party's position on Hunting, because reported in today's press was a deeply disheartening message from James Paice MP, who is the Conservative MP for South East Cambridgeshire, and Minister of State (Agriculture and Food), Environment,

Food and Rural Affairs. He has dismissed the prospect of any repeal of the hated Hunting Act in 2011, saying that with so many issues on its plate, the government cannot give the hunting issue sufficient priority to justify parliamentary time. And in the report I read, there was no assurance that repeal would come at all.

"Priority" is a pretty thin excuse, since most people believe that the repeal could consist of a two-line bill, or a one-line clause in a longer bill, and should take very little time. To be fair, I don't think many people in the hunting fraternity expected repeal next year. That is perhaps not simply because all reasonable people recognise that increasing the Overseas Aid Budget and urgently building more wind farms are vastly more important than rural concerns, but rather because the Conservative Party has been busy lowering expectations on the hunting issue. Some might think that the Party had cynically managed the hunting question to gain the support, and the votes, of the Countryside Alliance and of the 400,000+ people who marched in London to oppose the Ban in 2003. Now that the Party is in government, suddenly the issue looks less important.

But the government knows that radical steps need to be taken early in a government, or they end up in the long grass. The argument starts to be "We can't look at this divisive issue in the run-up to a General Election".

---

twitter

Shock-horror revelation! Some nights Tony Blair had a gin before dinner and a half bottle of wine with. So what? Who doesn't?

ABOVE: Here you can see my banner at the Fernie Hunt Team Chase as a horse and rider clear one of the formidable obstacles on the course. I am always amazed at how few fallers there are on this tough course.

I personally feel deeply ashamed of the delay. I have seen over the years the degree of support the Conservative Party has received from hunt supporters. Sometimes these people are natural conservatives. Some are largely apolitical, and are campaigning simply for their sport, trusting the promises that the Party has made. Just one example: I remember going up to Scarborough & Whitby in the 2005 general election to support my former MEP colleague, now MP, Robert Goodwill. We were canvassing in the dark, and in some of the most appalling weather I can remember. Howling wind and torrential rain. And the group campaigning consisted (so far as I can remember) of me, and Robert, and a bunch of hunt supporters. Frankly the weather was so bad that by myself I might have given up and gone home, but I kept going because the hunt supporters kept going.

We owe them one. We have made a clear promise, and we have to fulfil it. I for one won't feel able to hold up my head at countryside events until we do.

But it was not all bad news. In January 2011 UNESCO recognised falconry as a cultural icon. I was delighted and blogged accordingly.

This recognition came after a long and intensive campaign by practitioners of the sport from many countries, including especially the Middle East, but also from many European countries, the USA, Turkey and beyond. Representatives of the falconry organisations from sixteen of these countries, together with officers of FACE, the European Hunting

organisation, converged on the Strasbourg parliament on January 19th for a celebration, a colloquium on falconry, and a subsequent reception.

ABOVE: In January 2011 UNESCO recognised falconry as a cultural icon. The EU Parliament marked the event with an exhibition, which I visited along with Veronique Mathieu, a French Christian Democrat MEP.

The history of falconry can be traced back to around 2000 BC in the Middle East, making it about as old as hare coursing. It is believed to have been introduced into the UK in the Ninth Century, and in Mediaeval times became a popular sport and a status symbol. It was the sport of kings, and important folk loved to be painted while on horseback with a falcon on their wrist. While I say "Falcon", a range of raptors was used in the sport, and the choice of species conveyed social status. Gyrfalcons were well up the list, above peregrines, goshawks, and sparrow hawks — with the kestrel at the bottom, used and owned by the common man.

The real importance of this UNESCO recognition is the status it confers on hunting in general. In the East Midlands in particular, hunting is woven into the fabric of rural life, an unbroken thread of culture that binds man to his natural world. And if falconry is an intangible cultural heritage, then undoubtedly English fox-hunting is as well.

A Sceptic at Large

I understand why an EU superstate would be bad for Britain and bad for those people that I have the honour to represent. I am therefore sceptical of moves to create such a monstrosity. I understand why the science behind global climate change is deeply flawed and am therefore sceptical of arguments put forward that the science is settled. Likewise I am sceptical of political correctness for very sound reasons.

But there are times when my skeptical side comes out for no particular reason. I don't know why, but my political antennae twitch and I smell a rat. So I start digging. Sometimes I turn out to be correct to suspect that something is amiss. Other times I am not. But it is always interesting looking about for additional information – and sometimes you can turn up something quite bizarre.

Take, for instance, that dispute between Russia and Georgia back in 2008. Trouble had been brewing for years between the government of Georgia and the provinces of South Ossetia and Abkhazia, which would prefer not have been part of Georgia. The precise sequence of events is still rather murky even now, but in August a unit of the Georgian army deployed into South Ossetia and there was some bloodshed. The Russian army then invaded to "keep the peace" and overran much of Georgia before falling back into South Ossetia and Abkhazia.

Ever eager to posture on the world stage, the EU announced that it was sending a monitoring force to Georgia to keep an eye on the situation. I was startled to hear that the UK was going to be sending soldiers to take part and decided to do a bit of research. I did not like what I found and the following press story was the result.

MEP challenges EU plan for Georgia

The Foreign Secretary has announced that the UK will contribute to a so-called EU monitoring force which will deploy to Georgia on October 1. Under an agreement signed in Moscow and Tbilisi, Russian troops are expected to withdraw from the areas of Georgia that they occupy outside of South Ossetia and Abkhazia by October 10.

Roger Helmer the Conservative MEP for the East Midlands commented:

"Despite the announcements, it is totally unclear what nature this 'monitoring' force will assume. Some reports suggest the UK is planning to contribute police and non-uniformed military personnel. It seems we are planning to send British policemen to Georgia at a time when the public are worried about too few police on our streets at home.

"This particular EU mission is being carried out under the EU security and defence policy heading, and is being used very shamelessly to promote the need for a common defence policy.

"Russian troops should withdraw from all Georgian territory, including the disputed areas, and be replaced by an OSCE or UN force. An international investigation should be launched into the atrocities that are alleged to have taken place during the conflict. Meanwhile, the EU should focus its efforts on delivering the 500 million Euros of humanitarian aid which it has pledged to Georgia over the next three years, instead of distracting itself with promoting its own defence agenda."

One instance where I was at first sceptical but later supportive came during my June 2010 visit to South Korea as part of the EU Interparliamentary Delegation. I explained in a blog on 12th June.

EU Gateway? Or EU Exit Door?

On my visit to Seoul, I was interested to see that we were scheduled to visit something called the EU Gateway Exhibition, at the Coex Centre. Naturally I was initially concerned that this might be a typical piece of EU propaganda, and I approached it in a mood of scepticism. This mood was not much assuaged when I found that the programme had cost some tens of millions of euros, over two years in Seoul and seven in Japan.

However it turns out to be an apparently legitimate exercise in trade promotion, and if the EU offers British companies a subsidised opportunity to develop business in Japan and Korea (both difficult countries for Western businesses to approach cold), then we should be taking advantage of it. Some 58 companies from EU member-states had stands at the event, paying their own travel and subsistence but getting the stands and promotional support free. The sad thing was that while there were three companies from Latvia (population 2.2 million), there was none from the UK. I had hopes of a UK company when I bumped into Steve Bridges, who had been with the British Embassy when I was working in Korea in the early '90s, but the exhibitor he was now working with turned out to be Italian.

Naturally I enquired why there were no UK companies, and I was assured that the event had been promoted in the UK, that half a dozen companies had made tentative bookings, but all had cancelled as a result of the recession. A pity, because I heard anecdotal evidence that several of the companies exhibiting were pleased with their results and had found local agents or partners or customers.

However I heard a rather sad story from the European Chamber of Commerce in Seoul, who felt that they should have won the contract for

twitter

Better late than never: there's to be a badger cull. More common sense from the Coalition.

> **twitter** 🐦
> North Korea is so predictable. Shell the South & sink a warship, then offer talks on reuniting broken families. And pass the begging bowl.

organising the event. The contract in fact went to Eurochambres, the Brussels-based, Commission-funded NGO – which has little or no presence in Seoul. You have an interesting contrast between an in-country organisation of European businessmen in Seoul, with excellent local trade and government contacts, bidding against a Brussels-centric Eurochambres with good lobbying contacts in Brussels. So the Commission chooses to work with the top-down organisation close to home, rather than the bottom-up organisation that knows its way around Korea. Typical.

On balance, (and apart from the Eurochambres point), I decided that there was not a lot to criticise about the EU Gateway (though I should like to see a more formal analysis of results achieved). But somehow the very name of it stuck in my throat, and I couldn't resist Tweeting "EU Gateway? Many of my constituents would rather find an EU Exit Door!"

In 1975, long before I had any political ambitions at all, I went on a business visit to Barcelona and saw the Church of the Holy Family, designed by Antoni Gaudi back in 1883. The design for this church is widely hailed as

Gaudi's masterpiece with its 18 soaring spires, surrealistic sculptures and art noveau flourishes . When I first saw it, it was in a poor state. It had several of Gaudi's trade-mark towers, a bit of apse, and some sorry-looking, weathered fragments of wall which could have been an abandoned building project, or the remains of an ancient ruin. So far as I could see, the entire work-force consisted of two men, a wheelbarrow and a dog, and I decided that they could scarcely maintain what was there, never mind complete the project.

To say that I was sceptical about the chances of the masterpiece ever being completed would have been an understatement. But in 2008 I went back and blogged about what I found.

I recently made a pilgrimage to Barcelona to see Gaudi's masterwork, the Temple of the Holy Family, or the Eglisa de la Sagrada Familia, a building which has fascinated me for decades.

The 1992 Barcelona Olympics gave the project a huge boost, and I saw it again soon afterwards. The transformation was dramatic. The site was packed with cranes, heavy equipment, men in hard hats, and all the noise and bustle of an active construction site. But there was still a long way to go.

Today, large parts of the structure are complete, with a nave, side aisles, transepts and so on. There are walls on all sides, and the entire space is roofed.

Yet more needs to be done, especially on the South-East Front, and while the roof is in place, the huge central tower is only partly started. The interior is still filled with the noise and activity of a building site, but there is already extensive and stunning stained glass in the windows.

The Sagrada Familia is, depending on your point of view, either the grotesque nightmare of a designer who, if not intoxicated with narcotics, at least appeared to be hallucinating; or, alternatively, a mighty triumph of the human imagination, a splendid sui generis concept that bears no comparison with anything else in the world. I subscribe to the latter view.

The weekend before my visit the Sunday Telegraph ran its "My Kind of Town" feature on Barcelona, and said "There's no need to go inside the Sagrada Familia; you can get great views from the outside". They could scarcely be more wrong. Yes, there are great views from the outside, but the inside is stunning. Gaudi was inspired both by geometry and by natural forms. His forest of elegantly sculpted columns divide like tree branches to support the roof, and use profiles and contours that are entirely unique to this church. There are lifts up the towers allowing access to the narrow spiral staircases between their double walls, with amazing views across the city. No description does it justice: you have to see it.

The church occupies a city block in a square grid layout, and two adjacent blocks (NE and SW) are given over to public parks, one with an elegant lake. But sadly the other two (NW and SE) are covered with undistinguished but multi-storey modern buildings. The SE front of the church is already extending into the roadway, so the finished SE front will be only yards away from five-

BELOW: The Sagrada Familia designed by Antoni Gaudi is a mighty triumph of the human imagination, a splendid sui generis concept that bears no comparison with anything else in the world. I have seen this project at different times over the past 35 years and never cease to be amazed.

storey buildings. I just wish that the City Fathers of Barcelona had the courage, and the money, to take over those two city blocks and convert them to parks and plazas to complement the Church.

When I first saw the Church in 1975, I thought it would never be finished. Now, I have some hopes that I may live to see the day.

Some things you just don't criticise or question. Things like The Queen Mother (God Bless Her Memory); Motherhood and Apple Pie; and of course Public Lending Libraries. I can still remember the peace and quiet of public libraries that I used as a youngster in the fifties, and the slightly musty smell of the books. Public libraries exist in most places in the world and are widely regarded as an essential precondition for an educated and literate population.

One of the earliest public libraries was in our own East Midlands region. The Francis Trigge Chained Library of St. Wulfram's Church, Grantham, Lincolnshire was founded in 1598 by the rector of nearby Welbourne. It's estimated that by 1790, there were about six hundred rental and lending libraries in the UK, with a clientèle of some fifty thousand. The mid to late 18th century

---

twitter

Jim Paice: "The government has higher priorities than repealing the Hunting Act". So keeping our word to the countryside is not a priority?

---

saw a virtual epidemic of feminine reading as novels became more and more popular, but the foundations of the modern public library system were laid by the 1850 Public Libraries Act, which formalised rate-payer funding.

So no one but an anti-intellectual brute would question the necessity for public libraries, would they? Well maybe they would. In July 2010 I stuck my head over the parapet and suggested that maybe the best solution of 1850 needs a re-think 160 years on.

When libraries began, books were rare and expensive, and average wages were low. No average home was likely to buy any book, beyond (if they were lucky) a Family Bible. And generally speaking, apart from the rare travelling circus, and bear-baiting in the High Street, entertainment for the masses was hard to come by. Public libraries fulfilled a vital need. They provided access to reference books, to educational and improving books, and as novels became popular, access to entertainment. And for most people, they were virtually the only source of these things.

Compare today. Books are cheap. Even those on average or low incomes can afford a couple of paperbacks to read on the beach in Benidorm. I can almost hear the Librarians saying "Yes, but what about the Pensioners?". Good question. But in my experience, charity shops, street fairs, village fêtes, country shows and car boot sales offer a huge range of titles, second hand, sometimes for as little as 10p. Books are cheap, and everyone can afford them.

Books are no longer the first source of reference. In the old days, door-to-door salesmen would try to sell the Encyclopædia Britannica to lower-middle-class families who could ill-afford it, with the improbable claim that it would transform the kiddies' educational prospects. Now you can check any reference in seconds on Google, for nothing. My helpful observations above on the history of libraries are a case in point. No one needs libraries for reference.

Nor are books any more a primary source of entertainment. Let's face it: these days most entertainment in the home is from television, or increasingly from the Internet. Anyone who can afford a TV or a computer can afford a few books, but mostly they prefer audio-visual.

But what, I hear you cry, about education? What about the needs of children and students? But of course almost all educational institutions have libraries appropriate to the special needs of their students. That's important. But it's not the primary task of public libraries. Isn't it the case that children from homes with books do better at

---

twitter

Q: How is Belgium like Iraq? A: Neither country seems able to establish a credible and stable government.

---

school than those from homes without books? Yes it is true (though we should be very careful about the direction of cause and effect). But this fact marks a failure of the library system. If books in the home drove academic performance, and if libraries provided books for those homes that would otherwise be without them, we should not see any difference between book-homes and non-book-homes. The fact that the problem exists demonstrates that libraries are failing to solve it.

My heretical conclusion is that in the internet age, libraries are nice to have, but in an age of financial austerity, they're by no means essential. If it gets to be a choice between libraries and kidney dialysis, I'd rather fund dialysis.

I have always been rather sceptical about the merits of any art or literature or poetry or architecture produced after about 1910. My scepticism was rather reinforced in August 2010 during a short holiday in the West Country. I blogged on my return as follows.

Holiday Reminiscences

I've just returned from a few days in the West Country, and I've seen what I believe to be the greatest work of art I've ever been privileged to stand in awe of. Move over, Michelangelo's David and Beethoven's Ninth. Move over, Mona Lisa and Midsummer Night's Dream. I'm talking Edward Burne-Jones.

I've always admired Burne-Jones. Recently while I was attending a Freedom Association gig at Southampton University, I took the opportunity to visit Southampton Art Gallery to see Burne-Jones' Perseus cycle. In Wiltshire, on a cultural weekend focussed on the work of William Morris and his collaborators, I went (across the county boundary) to Buscot Park (National Trust, www.buscot-park.com), and there in the saloon I saw Burne-Jones' "Legend of the Briar Rose" cycle.

Burne-Jones painted four great canvasses illustrating the Sleeping Beauty legend, over a period of as long as twenty years. They represent "The

ABOVE: Constituency duties take up a good deal of the time of an MEP. Here Emma McClarkin, my fellow East Midlands Conservative MEP from 2009, and I attend an event promoting the arts in our East Midlands region.

Briar Wood", with the hero, sword-in-hand, viewing the remains of former knights-errant who have sought and failed to break the spell. Then "The Council Room", where the aged king sleeps, surrounded by courtiers, and, behind a lattice, soldiers (the lattice was of course a favourite theme of Morris). Third is "The Garden Court", where maidens sleep beside a well and a loom, their limbs reflected in the shiny marble floor (surely it would be dusty after a hundred years?). Fourth is "The Rose

Bower", with the Princess (modelled on the artist's fourteen-year-old daughter) asleep among her maidens.

Perhaps oddly, Burne-Jones stopped there. He did not attempt to show either the apotheosis of the story, the awakening, nor the wedding festivities that followed, preferring to leave those to the imagination of the viewer.

Just a few years later, Burne-Jones was staying at Kelmscott Manor, summer home of his friend and collaborator William Morris, and just a short walk across the fields from Buscot. So he decided to walk across and see his work in situ. Feeling that they were not hung to best advantage, he offered (apparently at no extra charge) to reorganise the display, providing a number of linking panels, and integrating the framing into a continuous frieze around three sides of the room.

Just as I am rather sceptical of modern artistic endeavours, I am also somewhat sceptical of modern theories on teaching history. History has always fascinated me and is of crucial importance in the modern world. If a nation does not understand its past it cannot understand itself. I blogged on the subject in January 2011.

A nation needs a narrative

And children need an intellectual hinterland, a shared infrastructure of the mind; and that should include a basic knowledge of English history. Not some thin gruel of cod-sociology, of the kind that has been imposed on our schools by the left-wing academic educationalists, but a real and gripping story of the real people who made England what it was, and what it is. Like it or not, history is made by great leaders, great men and women, and great deeds. If in doubt, just read again the speech which Queen Elizabeth 1st made to her troops at Tilbury before the Spanish Armada in 1588.

With unprecedented levels of immigration, we can hardly expect newcomers to integrate and to adopt our values if they have no idea who we are. And unless our own children know where we come from, they too will not know where they are, or where they're going, or why it matters.

I was struck by a recent news report suggesting that the great majority of children have no idea who the man is on top of Nelson's column, but many hazarding a guess came up with …. Nelson Mandela! They simply know nothing about the greatest naval commander of all time, the towering British hero of two hundred years ago, Horatio, Admiral Lord Nelson. And as

twitter

Good riddance to the Severn Barrage. It was rotten value compared to nuclear, gas or coal. It was intermittent, and damaging to wildlife.

twitter

Sir Gawain and the Green Knight: the Folio
Society edition is sumptuous, but the (much
cheaper) Tolkien translation is literature!

*for the Roman Horatio, in whose
honour Nelson was presumably named,
no doubt he is as far from their
awareness as the Neanderthals.*

*I find that those of my generation
have, at least in some measure, a shared
knowledge of key texts, of the Bible, and
Shakespeare, and Dickens, and the
great poets. Familiar quotations form
part of the bric-à-brac, the small
change, of a well-stocked mind. Yet they
are largely unfamiliar to the younger
generation — even to the sort of very
bright and well-educated young people
who come to work as assistants in the
European parliament.*

*But for those concerned that their
children or grandchildren should know
more about our history, let me
recommend "Our Island Story", by
H.E. Marshall, first published in the
Edwardian twilight in 1905, before the
word "sociology" had been invented. It
has been bravely republished recently
(2005) by Civitas and Gore Park
Publishing. This book has been
commended to me a couple of times by
my good colleague Dan Hannan, but
I've been a bit dilatory about sending
for it. Now I have it. My copy is
destined for my grandsons, but I've been
flicking through the pages in the
meantime.*

*The book makes no attempt to
provide a complete account or analysis
of English history. Designed for
children, it takes key events — iconic
events — from British history, and
presents them as exciting short stories —
with illustrations apt to the tales, and in
the style of 1905. We have Boadicea
(and no revisionary nonsense about
Boudicca). We have Alfred and the
cakes; Hereward the Wake; the White
Ship; Thomas à Beckett; The Field of
the Cloth of Gold; Drake playing at
bowls on Plymouth Ho! and thumbing
his nose at the Armada; and of course,
the great Admiral Lord Nelson. Each
story is told in a few pages, suitable for
bed-time reading for children, and
guaranteed to excite a life-long interest
in our history.*

*There will be cynics and
curmudgeons and kill-joys who will
point out the inaccuracies. In all
probability, Alfred never burned any
cakes, and Robert the Bruce never
watched a spider. Probably the story of
Drake and the game of bowls is
apocryphal. But to complain in those
terms is to miss the point. These stories
are part of our national narrative; part
of the heritage and birthright of every
Englishman (and woman). They may
not be historically accurate, but in a
deeper and mythic sense they are true,
and our children and grandchildren
deserve to share them.*

History and art came together during
a visit to the Palace of Westminster to see
my old friend and colleague Chris

twitter

China's bullying of third countries over the Nobel Prize is disgraceful. They should be ashamed of themselves.

Heaton-Harris – formerly MEP for the East Midlands and now MP for Daventry. I blogged about the event immediately.

The Kings of England lifting up their swords

I've always been a great admirer of the equestrian statue of Richard the First, Coeur de Lion — Lionheart — in Old Palace Yard in front of the Palace of Westminster. It lifts the spirit. The sun was shining from a clear blue sky, the Palace looked wonderful — like a real parliament — and I couldn't resist the temptation to take a picture.

The statue was first commissioned in clay for the 1851 Great Exhibition. It was designed by the Italian sculptor Baron (Pietro) Carlo Giovanni Battista Marochetti (1805-1867). I love public art and sculpture, but at the risk of offending my good colleague Martin Callanan MEP (who represents the North East) I have to admit that I prefer Victorian heroics to the Angel of the North.

The statue of Richard was greatly admired in 1851, by John Ruskin amongst others, and a permanent bronze version was subsequently made,

funded for £5000 by public subscription. It has recently been refurbished and looks a million dollars (not a bad return on £5000).

It always puts me in mind of those lines of James Elroy Flecker:

Surely for us, as for those nobly dead,
The Kings of England, lifting up their swords,
Shall gather at the Gates of Paradise.

These days, of course, it is not kings that lift up swords to protect our nation, but more humble folk armed with rifles, grenades and pistols who sally forth to fight the foe. I was reminded of this in September 2010 when I visited Spalding, Lincolnshire. As I have already written, I have always been rather sceptical about the merits of any art or literature or poetry or architecture produced after about early 20th Century, which is perhaps why I'm a great fan of Sir Edwin Lutyens. At the time of my visit I was moved to blog as follows:

Lutyens started his career in the dying years of the 19th century, and became famous in the Edwardian Sunset for his Surrey vernacular country houses, often working with the landscape gardener Gertrude Jekyll. A Lutyens/Jekyll

twitter

Dog walking: The Green Lanes are white with fallen flecks of may-blossom, like a pointilliste painting by Seurat.

country house became the aspiration of the affluent upper-middle classes. He went on to civic and commercial architecture, and after the First World War, sadly, found much of his attention taken up with War Memorials.

In a peripatetic life I've been privileged to visit many of his buildings. The Rashtrapati Bhavan, or Viceroy's Palace, in New Delhi; the British Ambassador's Residence in Washington; and the magnificent arched War Memorial at Thiepval on the Somme. I've been to many of his buildings in the UK, from Lindisfarne Castle in Northumberland to Castle Drogo in Devon.

I have known for some time that there was a Lutyens War Memorial in Spalding, but I'd never had the chance to find it. Last Friday, ahead of the South Holland Supper Club event, I found myself in Spalding with an hour on my hands, and enquired in the South Holland Centre, where a very helpful lady gave me directions. The memorial is in the park at Ayscoughee Hall, just a short walk from the town centre across the river via a rather attractive pedestrian bridge.

BELOW: At the East Midlands Food Festival in October 2010 I made a point of supporting our local quality food producers. Here I am with Simon Jones who makes the excellent Lincolnshire Poacher Cheese.

A three-arched pavilion structure, it faces a rectangular lake which Lutyens would have no doubt called a "tank", and is surrounded by remarkable curvilinear clipped yew hedges. It is about as close to perfect as a War Memorial can be. If you're in Spalding, be sure to visit it. I hope to be able to get to Spalding for the Remembrance Service at the Memorial later this year.

"As close to perfect as a War Memorial can be," I wrote. I was right. Lutyen's monument is inscribed with the words "Their Name Liveth for Evermore". And so they should.

On a quite different note, one of the on-going nonsenses in Brussels has been the old story about straight bananas – how the EU imposes rules on fruit and veg that are entirely cosmetic and have nothing to do with how wholesome or tasty the food may be. As a result vast quantities of perfectly good food are destroyed because the banana is too curvy, the apple too small or the asparagus too green. Those who praise the EU and its works have for years bleated about these stories and accused us EU sceptics of making the stories up. So it was with some delight that in November 2008 the EU itself proved us right. At the time I put up the following on my website:

Straight Bananas

Finally the EU has come clean and admitted that it really did have rules on straight bananas. For years, supporters of the EU have talked about straight bananas as a "euro-myth", a story so ridiculous that only bad people seeking to debunk the EU could have told such dreadful lies.

Odd, then, that the EU Commission has just announced that it is to ditch a whole raft of rules on straight bananas, curved cucumbers and wonky vegetables. Of course euro-realists have been pointing out for years that the European Union really does have regulations on straight bananas (Directive No 2257/94 of 16 September 1994). But somehow the euro-myth story stuck, and the left-wing press never grasped the truth.

This really matters, especially in times of economic hardship. Perfectly good fruit -- apples that were too small, pears with minor surface blemishes -- were thrown away, or became cattle feed, because of European rules. Meantime hard-pressed housewives counting the pennies would have been happy to buy small apples for small children, or for apple pies.

At last they've done the sensible thing -- that they should have done years ago. Indeed these daft and

twitter 🐦

Well done the BBC (!). A half-hour programme this a.m. on the Irish Clonmel Hare-Coursing Meeting. We need to get back the Waterloo Cup!

damaging regulations should never have reached the statute book. But the lesson has not been learned. We may have cancelled a few silly rules, but we create far more new ones every month. EU regulation is costing every family in Britain hundreds of pounds a year, and making us all poorer.

I wrote too soon. The wretched EU has the capacity to take even a hardened Sceptic like me by surprise sometimes. In February 2010, things took a new turn for the worse as I explained on my website.

Wonky fruit rules are bananas!

Fruit and veg are under the EU spotlight again as Spanish MEPs have moved to get the EU to re-impose its ban on misshapen fruit and vegetables. The Spanish amendments, if passed, could spell misery for local farmers whose fruit and veg might not necessarily pass a beauty contest but whose flavour and quality is uncompromised.

To try and stop stores selling perfectly decent food simply because of its shape and size is morally unjustifiable, especially when we are worried about global food supplies and are still in recovering from an economic downturn. I thought common sense had finally prevailed when the European Commission relaxed the rules.

Our farmers were grateful too as it meant they could sell their perfectly good

twitter

Eric Pickles defends English county names against the Post Office. He's right. History, culture, tradition, location and identity matter.

and often better quality produce. If the Spanish MEPs get their way, we could see the re-introduction of the ludicrous bendy banana rules. My Conservative colleagues and I will bitterly oppose the move on behalf of local farmers.

Consumers will decide what they want. Let the market decide, not the European Parliament."

It was not only farms that were falling under ridiculous EU rules. Take those most harmless of folk, the English angler. I explained on my website in January 2009 what was afoot.

Recreational fishing to fall within the Common Fisheries Policy?

The EU Commission has proposed a regulation that changes the Common Fisheries Policy. Article 47 of the regulation would require recreational fishermen to register their boats, and whatever they catch would be counted against the fisheries quota for that country. Each country will also be required to allocate what share of its quota for each fish species will be available for commercial and recreational fisheries use.

The proposal is expected to begin its passage through the European Parliament later this month, with a final vote expected in April. Conservatives will be submitting amendments removing recreational fishing from the regulation.

Recreational fishing is a simple pleasure that would become a bureaucratic nightmare if these plans become law. This kind of draconian approach would do very little to assist in the recovery of fish stocks, yet it will cause a great deal of damage to tourism and the whole fishing sport.

If the European Union is serious about acting to protect fish stocks in the EU, it should launch a fundamental overhaul of the CFP, not target an ancient hobby. Not content with destroying our North Sea fisheries. Now, they want a go at our rivers as well.

If the EU is a worthy target for my scepticism, so too are the growing number of wealthy and intransigent pressure groups collectively known as NGOs (Non-Governmental Organisations). These NGOs have their origins in worthy charities supported by public donations, but many are now bigoted pressure groups funded by the taxpayer (often via the EU). Since becoming an MEP I have learned to be wary of their motives, sceptical of their claims and reluctant to get involved with them. I should add here that the Campaign for the Protection of Rural England (CPRE) is actually one of the better NGOs if for no other reason than that most of its income still derives from voluntary donations – there are far worse offenders – it is just that this incident sums up so much that is wrong with the system.

I blogged about an encounter with an NGO in July 2010.

The Benefits of "Undergrounding"

I have just been made privy to some correspondence between a constituent and the Campaign for the Protection of Rural England (CPRE), in which the CPRE (a certain Dustin Benton, who works on "the CPRE's climate and energy policy") sets out a pro-wind-farm policy. Genuflecting to the conventional view, Mr. Benton says that "the threat that climate change poses to the beauty and character of England's landscapes justifies the development of a wide range of renewables, including on and offshore wind", and adds for good measure "We believe that wind power, especially offshore, where the wind blows more strongly and where wind farms can be more easily sited to reduce visual impact, should make a significant contribution to the provision of vitally needed renewable electricity".

twitter

Heard a piece by early Baroque composer Johann Joseph Fux (no ribald jokes, please!) last night. Excellent stuff -- worth looking out for.

I have written to Mr. Benton pointing out that this seems rather at odds with the expressed view of the Chief Executive of CPRE, Shaun Spiers, who is quoted as saying that "We may come to see wind turbines as the redundant relics of our compulsion to do something" (though they now claim he meant that wind turbines would be redundant unless we also did a load of other stuff). I think that Mr. Spiers was right first time, and that Mr. Benton is wrong.

But I was struck by another remark in Mr. Benton's e-mail: "CPRE's pylons campaign is calling for pylons to be undergrounded in nationally designated landscapes. We believe that large pylons and other intrusive forms of built development harm the character of areas that are designated for their natural beauty".

In my note to Mr. Benton, I have said "I am struck by the obvious benefits to landscape and the environment of having pylons "undergrounded" (a new verb in my lexicon). I think that onshore wind turbines would also be much more acceptable if they were undergrounded".

Now there's a solution we could all applaud.

Talking of wind farms, I have been involved in campaigns against several of these ghastly things across the East Midlands. My blog in October 2010 about the Sproxton Wind Turbine

twitter

Environmentalism plus Localism: Yesterday, walking the dog, I collected twenty-three aluminium drinks cans from the roadsides for recycling.

Proposal is given here as it is typical of many. With wind farm proposals the most important thing is to remain highly sceptical about the claims made by those who want to build them. I wrote to the Melton Mowbray Council on the proposal as follows.

I write to support those local residents of Sproxton who have objected to this proposal, and to register my own objection as an MEP representing the area.

I have studied the report on this proposal by Planning Officer Mrs. Jennifer Wallace, and I am concerned at the apparently casual way in which it dismisses all objections. For example, the Environmental Health Officer has studied "information on noise levels" (presumably provided by the applicant or the turbine manufacturer) and concludes that "the turbine will not be audible in the village". Since the village is no more than 200 yards away, with dwellings within a quarter mile, this strains credibility. Would the applicant be amenable to a condition in any future planning consent requiring the turbine to be inaudible in the village?

twitter

News Reports. Compare & contrast: gloom & doom at the Biodiversity Conference in Nagoya; great news on the recovery of UK otter populations

The report dismisses the issue of footpaths as "the turbine is some distance from recorded public bridleways". That may be, but it is very close to roads which are widely used by horse-riders, and I understand that the local equestrian community is very concerned. Turbines with their noise, flicker, reflection and strobe effects can be a serious disturbance to horses and therefore a danger to riders. I note that the amended plan takes the turbine nearer to the road.

The local Cricket Club has submitted a well-researched and well-argued objection, which has been dismissed in the same casual manner.

The report says "there is no evidence to show that the proposed turbine is not viable". But there is no evidence to show that it is viable. Typically on-shore turbines deliver only around 25% of their rated capacity, small turbines are less efficient than larger ones, and Leicestershire has some of the lowest average wind speeds in the country. It should be incumbent on the Planning Committee to satisfy itself that the intermittent trickle of electricity which would be provided by this turbine justifies the significant negative local

impacts. This turbine would be an example of "gesture politics", creating the impression of action on the environment while achieving a trivial real contribution.

I fear that the credibility of the planning process is called into question by this cavalier dismissal of objections. We have a new government committed to localism. It is time to pay more attention to the concerns of local people.

You will be aware that Scotland has wisely created planning advice calling for a 2km set-back for new turbines. Local authorities in the UK are free to introduce similar measures, and (as the Sproxton Cricket Club cogently argue in their letter) the neighbouring County of Lincolnshire has done so. It is difficult to see why the residents of Sproxton should enjoy a lower standard of protection than the citizens of Scotland or Lincolnshire. I urge you to reject this application.

Yours sincerely,

Roger Helmer MEP.

I should add that the Melton Mowbray Council was stung by my reference to "casual way in which it dismisses all objections" and took me through their response in some detail. But I was left with the impression that they had followed due process with great diligence while failing to engage with the reality of residents' concerns.

Peering into the Future

Where is the EU going?

"Forecasting is difficult, especially about the future". This wonderful line has been attributed to many sources, not least Yogi Berra, Dan Quayle and Victor Borge. Or I suppose it could have been Woody Allen (I love his line "I'm not afraid of dying -- I just don't wanna be there when it happens").

Forecasting is indeed difficult. I love to read the predictions of economic journalists (and to hear the Today Programme's racing tips), but of course if they had a better-than-average success rate, they'd be coining-in money on the stock exchange (or at the races), not offering their tips to the credulous.

So I start with a caution that applies to all predictions. Nonetheless, I think it's worth drawing out some useful trends that suggest where the EU might be going in the future.

A shrinking economy

There are a number of long-term projections from highly respected institutions which forecast that in terms of share of the world economy, emerging Asia will increase over the medium term, the USA will roughly hold share – and the EU will decline.

A 2005 report from the UK Treasury showed the US share of global output holding steady at around 20% between 1980 and 2015. China and India together increased from 6% to a stunning 27% -- while the EU declined from 26% to 17%. Goldman Sachs are forecasting that by 2050, China will have 28% of world GDP, the USA 13%, India 12% and Euroland a paltry 8%, barely half its current share of global GDP.

There are two major factors driving GDP and share of world trade, and they are firstly population, and secondly productivity. In the case of population, we can make rather reliable predictions, because demographic changes move slowly and are predicated in large part on existing birth-rate trends.

China faces demographic problems, partly as a result of the one-child policy, although that is being relaxed. But China's problem is a couple of decades behind Europe, where catastrophically low birth-rates are well below replacement levels in many countries -- even in those Catholic countries that traditionally had higher birth-rates. So a large part of the EU's decline is already set in place.

America on the other hand is a much younger country with a high level of (predominantly young) immigration, so it will not face the same demographic problems.

Then there is the question of productivity. Europe has had a stubborn problem of productivity, and has generally been unable to match progress seen in the US. China as a rapidly developing nation has much more headroom to increase productivity with new investment.

So the EU starts in a bad place, but

(as you will have seen in the earlier parts of this book) it also seems to have a regulatory death-wish. It insists on piling ever more regulation on industry, reducing efficiency and adding to unit labour costs with ever harsher administrative requirements. The Working Time Directive, the Agency Workers Directive, parental leave, health and safety, REACH (the chemicals directive), each adds hugely to the costs of doing business in the EU. Plus of course carbon taxes, emissions trading and a cat's cradle of regulatory burdens designed to "mitigate climate change". These measures add billions to industry's costs, and devastate competitiveness.

Many of these measures seem perversely designed to drive business and jobs and investment out of the EU altogether – and ironically, to drive it to foreign jurisdictions with (frequently) lower environmental standards. So we lose the business, and potentially increase the pollution at the same time.

Recent reports suggest that there is massive environmental pollution taking place in China as part of the rare earth extraction necessary for (inter alia) building Chris Huhne's wind turbines, and electric cars. And of course most of Huhne's "Green Jobs" – where they happen at all – will happen in China.

There was the Tobacco Directive, which moved the production of higher strength cigarettes out of Nottingham (Imperial Tobacco) and offshore to Bangladesh or Brazil.

There was the battery hen regulation that moved a huge swathe of egg production from the EU to the Ukraine, India, Thailand and Taiwan – so EU farmers lost out, and (on balance) so did the chickens.

There are new anti-discrimination proposals on pensions and financial services that could lead to EU consumers buying insurance off-shore.

There are the environmental constraints on ship-breaking which have led to ships being broken up on beaches in India where the work-force includes children in flip-flops – with no safety equipment at all.

But the biggest problem is the plethora of measures designed to curb CO_2 emissions. These have made the EU a terrible place for energy-intensive industries like glass and ceramics, metals, cement, and paper.

The democratic deficit

My colleague Dan Hannan MEP has a catch-phrase that I have shamelessly plundered and quoted: "The EU is making us poorer, and less democratic, and less free". In the first part of this chapter I have sketched the reasons why the EU is making us poorer. I mean, of course, poorer than we would otherwise be – not poorer than we were twenty years ago.

Apologists for the EU project like to quote large increases over the years in standards of living in the EU, and increases in trade. They cheerfully ignore the fact that the rest of the world (broadly speaking) has done as well or better. The test is not whether prosperity has grown in the EU, but whether the policies and institutions of the EU have given Europe any advantage compared to the rest of the world. The answer is clearly "No". We have seen how the EU is declining in terms of share of world trade.

But less democratic? How can I, as an elected MEP, say that? Surely democracy is all about voting, and EU citizens get the right to vote? But there are fundamental reasons why the EU is not, and cannot be, democratic. For a start, almost nobody ever gets to be an MEP unless they have at some stage gone to a Party meeting and indicated an interest in becoming a candidate. And what sort of people might do that? Overwhelmingly, people who are enthusiasts for the European project.

There are of course some exceptions. I and one or two Conservatives stood for election because we were appalled at the way the EU, and Britain's relationship with it, were developing. And candidates for rejectionist parties like UKIP are frankly and openly opposed to the EU project. But the great majority of MEPs are euro-enthusiasts.

There was an excellent illustration of this mis-match between elected MEPs and their constituents when we voted on a report welcoming the EU Constitution (later transmogrified into the Lisbon Treaty). The great majority of French and Dutch MEPs voted for the report. But in subsequent referenda in both countries, the people (God bless 'em) rejected the Constitution by a significant margin.

It seems that voters are starting to catch up with this mis-match. In the past, they simply voted red or blue or yellow in Euro-elections, just as they would in General Elections. But the rapid rise in the UKIP vote in euro-elections (they came second, ahead of Labour, in 2009) suggests that voters have realised that none of the major parties reflects their view on the EU, and have reacted accordingly.

Ethnographic boundaries

But there is a much more fundamental reason why the EU is not, and cannot be, democratic. You can invite any arbitrary group of people to vote. And you can count the votes. But unless the group of people you start with has some kind of common identity and coherence, your process is not democracy. It is no more than arithmetic.

Let me offer you a couple of my favourite quotes on this subject. John Stuart Mill said that "Among a people without fellow-feeling, especially if they read and speak different languages, the united public opinion, necessary to the working of representative government, cannot exist".

Then there was Enoch Powell. (I know that Conservatives are not supposed to mention Enoch Powell, but he was a political giant and a towering intellect, and I am happy and proud to quote him). He said that democracy was only legitimate amongst a people who shared enough in common, in terms of language, culture, history and economic interests, that they were prepared to accept governance at each others' hands.

Consider the map of Africa. Many of

the boundaries between countries are straight lines. I imagine Victorian worthies sitting in the Chancelleries of Europe, ruler in hand, and drawing lines on a map, quite regardless of topological features or tribal loyalties. I believe that many of the problems of Africa result directly from these artificial boundaries that bear no relation to the identities and aspirations of their citizens.

Tribes who could have been good neighbours if they had had a degree of separation and independence find themselves vying and fighting for supremacy within boundaries that they never agreed.

The European Union fails both the John Stuart Mill test and the Enoch Powell test. We do not have the common language, still less the common public opinion, which Mill said were necessary conditions for representative government. We do not have enough in common to "accept governance at each others' hands".

So can we have a democratic Europe? Yes we can. But only if we have what Dan Hannan calls "ethnographic boundaries". Only if we have independent, democratic nations, trading and cooperating together, but not making a pretence of cross-border democracy, which leads directly to the sort of unresponsive, unaccountable, technocratic and corporatist institutions we see in Brussels. It leads to an alienation of the people from their government.

So we come to a fundamental rule of democratic governance. The boundaries we create, and within which we conduct elections, must reflect the identity and aspirations of the citizens. That is why I'm happy to vote for a County Council in Leicestershire, or an MP to represent me in Westminster, but I do not believe we should have an elected assembly for the East Midlands – or for the EU. The European parliament, like so much else in the EU, is designed to give a false impression of democratic accountability where none exists.

What future for the euro?

Ever since I became actively engaged in politics as a candidate – from 1998 – I have argued that the concept of a single currency for the EU was fatally flawed, and that Britain should not join. The arguments which I and others used then, and which have since been vindicated, are well known.

The euro-zone is not, in economists' terms an "optimal currency area".

A currency area should not be too small, or the costs of exchange will become disproportionate. A separate currency for (say) the Isle of Wight might yield ideal monetary policy and interest rates for the Island. But the administrative hassle of travelling and trading in a separate currency would be too great a cost to bear.

There is no theoretical limit to how big an optimal currency area might be – after all, the USA is quite large, both geographically and economically. But an area can be too diverse to cope with a single currency, and this is exactly the problem – which we predicted and we now witness at first hand – in Europe.

I'm often asked how a single currency can be a problem in Europe when it works perfectly well in the USA. And I like to get the question, because if you understand why it works in the States, you understand why it won't work in Europe.

There are three necessary conditions for a single currency to succeed. The first is labour mobility. If you're out-of-work in Pittsburgh, you can get on a Greyhound bus to New York or San Francisco. Yet there's less labour mobility within EU member states than there is in the USA – never mind labour mobility between member-states.

Then there's the question of federal fund transfers between rich and poor areas. This is achieved in the US through a range of federal programmes which redistribute funds. There are various programmes in the EU that might have a similar effect – the Structural Funds, for example. But the total EU budget is only around 1% of GDP, whereas credible economic estimates suggest that a minimum of six to eight percent would be needed to balance rich and poor areas in a single currency zone. There is no way this money can or should be raised in an EU which is already grossly over-taxed.

And thirdly there is political will. Americans all salute the same flag, and are therefore mostly happy to see their tax dollars helping the worse-off. That degree of altruism is unlikely to apply when the beneficiaries are in "distant countries of which we know little".

In assessing the prospects for the single currency, we also anticipated asymmetric shocks – external events which would have hugely different consequences in different euro-zone countries. The obvious example would have been oil price changes where some member-states had oil production but most did not.

In the event, though, the biggest challenge in the eurozone proved to be the divergence of productivity rates and unit labour costs between successful economies like Germany and less successful ones like Greece – coupled with excessive government debt, accompanied by a degree of false accounting.

The irony is that before the launch of the euro, the soon-to-be-eurozone used differential interest rates to achieve convergence. It never seems to have crossed their minds that the euro implied the same interest rates across the eurozone. They could no longer use differential rates to drive convergence, and the result – obvious with hindsight – was massive divergence.

There is only one way for a country like Greece to regain its competitiveness within the eurozone, and that is for it to undergo massive, grinding, internal deflation. Big real-terms reductions in salaries, benefits and government spending. This might work in economic terms, but it is probably not deliverable in political terms in a democracy.

My view is that the bail-out mechanisms proposed, rather tentatively, by the EU will do no more than delay the day of reckoning.

So Greece (and perhaps Portugal and Ireland) faces really only two choices. It

could remain within the eurozone but renege on its obligations. Let's make it easier with a euphemism. It needs an orderly, managed debt restructuring. Or a haircut. But it would be a huge blow to the credibility of the euro, and the EU, if one or more eurozone states were to default.

Or Greece could leave the euro. Its "New Drachma" would immediately devalue by at least 30%, increasing its external obligations proportionately. But then we've already agreed that Greece will have to default (sorry, restructure). So on balance, I think Greece would do better to go for the permanent solution of leaving the eurozone, rather than make a temporary

ABOVE: On 17th March 2011 I went to No.10 Downing Street with my lovely wife Sara for a reception given by the Prime Minister for Conservative MEPs. Recalling that classic photo of Harold Wilson when he was a boy, I joked "When I grow up I want to be Prime Minister".

adjustment which might well need to be repeated down the road.

Clearly any default by the PIGS (Portugal/Ireland/Greece/Spain) will have interesting consequences for European and other banks with exposure to these nations' debts.

So I believe that the most likely outcome will be that the euro will survive, but that some countries will leave it. And when that process is complete, the rump euro may be viable – or at least more viable than it is now. The other big question is, which countries would remain in the euro? Some commentators have suggested that France might not survive long-term in a currency union with Germany. We shall see.

And the EU itself?

Cast your mind back to 1985, and consider the USSR. Many of us would have said then that the USSR could not survive. It would submerge under the weight of its own internal contradictions and inefficiencies. We believed that intellectually, but did we really believe it in our hearts? Did we not feel that the USSR was monolithic? That it was a part, however objectionable, of the world's permanent global architecture? Weren't we honestly surprised when the wall came down? Of course we were.

I think we're getting to the same place with the EU. As a eurosceptic myself, I believe that such an inefficient, corrupt, anti-democratic system of governance cannot survive. We see public opinion going ever more negative. We see the fury over irrational European rulings, like Votes-for-Convicts. Surely the whole rotten structure must collapse? Surely it is beyond reform, and needs to be put out of its misery?

We see the logic of these arguments, yet we are so accustomed to our new status as an offshore province in a new nation called Europe that we don't believe it in our hearts. We are told that all the global trends are towards larger groupings. The EU's leaders have not-so-private dreams of global governance (and what an Orwellian nightmare that would be).

Yet there is a strong counter-trend. The USSR was an attempt to set up a common polity with centralised policies that rode rough-shod over the identities and aspirations of ancient nations. And it failed. In a smaller way the same can be said of Yugoslavia. And within old established countries we see a fissiparous trend. Not just devolution for Scotland and Wales, but independence movements in Catalonia and the Basque country, and a strong separatist tendency in Belgium. Indeed Belgium is in some ways a metaphor for the EU – an illogical grouping with no national or democratic rationale.

Take heart. The USSR in various incarnations lasted around 70 years, from the Russian Revolution to the fall of the Berlin Wall. The EU (also in various incarnations) can be said to have started in 1957. If it matches the USSR in terms of longevity, we could see the wheels come off in 2027.

Cecil Rhodes said that the greatest prize in the lottery of life was to be born an Englishman. I was born an Englishman, and a free man in a free country, but a country that has since become an offshore province of the European Union. And now they tell me that I'm a "citizen of the European Union". I never asked to be an EU citizen. I never agreed to be an EU citizen. All I ask is to be a free man in a free country again.

"I am sceptical of grand schemes to remake the world"

David Cameron, Leader of the Conservative Party, speaking on the 5th Anniversary of the 9/11 attacks on the World Trade Centre in New York.